FLOWERS *for* TENNESSEE

FLOWERS *for* TENNESSEE

Judy Lowe

Nashville, Tennessee
A Division of Thomas Nelson, Inc.
www.ThomasNelson.com

Published by Cool Springs Press, a Division of Thomas Nelson, Inc.,
P.O. Box 141000, Nashville, Tennessee, 37214.

First printing 2004
Printed in the United States of America
10 9 8 7 6 5 4 3 2 1

Managing Editor: Mary Morgan
Horticulture Editor: Michael Wenzel, Atlanta Botanical Garden
Copyeditor: Michelle Adkerson
Designer: Bill Kersey, Kersey Graphics
Production Artist: S.E. Anderson

On the cover: Viola, photographed by Thomas Eltzroth

Visit the Thomas Nelson website at www.ThomasNelson.com

Table *of* Contents

How To Use This Book

Each entry in this guide provides you with information about a plant's particular characteristics, habits, and basic requirements for active growth as well as my personal experience and knowledge of the plant. I include the information you need to help you realize each plant's potential. Only when a plant performs at its best can one appreciate it fully. You will find such pertinent information as mature height and spread, bloom period and colors (if any), sun and soil preferences, water requirements, fertilizing needs, pruning and care, and pest information.

Sun Preferences

Symbols represent the range of sunlight suitable for each plant. Some plants can be grown in more than one range of sun, so you will sometimes see more than one sun symbol.

Full Sun

Part Sun/Shade

Full Shade

Additional Benefits

Many plants offer benefits that further enhance their appeal. The following symbols indicate some of the more important additional benefits:

 **Attracts Butterflies**

 **Attracts Hummingbirds**

 **Produces Edible Fruit**

 **Has Fragrance**

 **Produces Food for Birds and Wildlife**

 **Drought Resistant**

 **Suitable for Cut Flowers or Arrangements**

 **Long Bloom Period**

 **Native Plant**

 **Supports Bees**

 **Good Fall Color**

 **Provides Shelter for Birds**

Complementary Plants

For many of the entries, I provide landscape design ideas as well as suggestions for companion plants to help you achieve striking and personal gardening results from your garden. This is where I find the most enjoyment from gardening.

Recommended Selections

This section describes specific cultivars or varieties that I have found particularly noteworthy. Give them a try.

50 Great Flowers *for* Tennessee

Flowers are the jewels of the landscape and are what come to mind when most people think of gardening. With their wide variety of shapes, colors, textures, fragrance, even life cycles, they offer endless opportunities to create appealing combinations that delight all the senses. We are fortunate in Tennessee to be able to grow many different types of flowers. It's cold enough in winter for perennials such as peonies that must have a cold, dormant season in order to thrive. And it's warm enough in summer for plants that will not survive the cold—but love the heat—to put on a beautiful show for months on end. By combining these two types of flowers, our gardens can be gorgeous from March through October and sometimes beyond.

Coreopsis

Life Cycles of Flowers

In this book, I refer to flowers as either annuals or perennials. Technically, annuals are plants that grow, set seed, and die in one season, although we also use the term for any plant that will not survive our winters outdoors. Perennials are plants that live at least several years, and sometimes many years, with their foliage usually dying away and disappearing over winter, then sprouting again in spring. Tropical plants, such as datura, are treated as annuals in Tennessee, although they are perennial in climates such as south Florida's. And some annuals—cosmos come to mind—will self-seed, meaning they scatter their seeds around, so new plants appear season after season.

It isn't necessary to know exactly which horticultural category a flower falls into in order to enjoy it and succeed with it. The important things you need to know are whether it will winter over or not and how long it will stay in bloom. Annuals and most tropicals bloom for months, while perennials may stay in bloom only a few weeks. Many perennials have attractive foliage, though, and can play useful roles in the garden even when not in bloom.

Selecting Flowers

When selecting flowers for your garden, consider several factors:

- ***Planting conditions.*** Check the light, soil, and water conditions where you plan to plant. Most annuals are sun lovers. If you have many trees in your yard, look for flowers that prefer shade. Only a few plants will grow in poor soil, so work up your soil to 8 to 12 inches deep, if possible, add organic matter (such as finely shredded bark, rotted leaves, rotted manure, or compost), and mix it in thoroughly. Remove all grass and weeds, including roots, before working the soil.
- ***Color.*** Choose colors that coordinate with your house and with other plantings in the yard. Some gardeners like gardens of all one color while others enjoy combining colors. White and light colors are especially nice where you can see them in the evening, around the deck or patio, for example.
- ***Mature height.*** Flowers come in heights from a few inches to several feet, although most annuals grow to about a foot tall. You'll want a combination of heights, so look for plants that vary. In general, it's best to put lower-growing plants at the front of the garden, with mid-sized plants behind, and tall ones at the back.

Dianthus

Hosta

Culture Basics

Devoting the time in the beginning to do a really good job of improving your soil and removing weeds will pay off huge dividends down the road. Beyond that, flowers need water, fertilizer, dead-heading (picking off the blossoms that are past their prime in order to keep the plant from putting energy into producing seeds), unless you want the plant to self-seed, and a careful eye for disease or insect problems.

Since annuals generally bloom heavily for so long, they may need more fertilizer than perennials do. Over-fertilizing perennials can cause the stems to become weak and floppy. If you've done a good job of adding organic matter to your soil, perennials will need little if any added fertilizer. If you are mixing annuals and perennials together, one way to handle their different needs is to use a slow-release fertilizer in the planting holes for annuals, or, sprinkle them every few weeks with a water-soluble fertilizer.

Watering and weeding are essential for all flowers. Plants need about one inch of water per week, so use your rain gauge to tell you when to water. And do so thoroughly and deeply, all at one time, rather than sprinkling lightly every day. Deep watering encourages deep roots, making the plants more drought resistant.

Ageratum

Ageratum houstonianum

A Blue Annual for the Front of the Flower Bed

Low-growing ageratum is a staple in my yard. I like the mounded shape of the dwarf varieties, and the fuzzy little flowers last a long time with regular watering and deadheading. Not often available from nurseries, taller ageratum cultivars can be grown from seed. They make nice cut flowers and are great for a red, white, and blue color scheme.

Top Reasons to Plant

- Blooms all summer
- Neat, pretty edger for taller flowers
- Attractive, fuzzy texture to blooms
- Tolerates light shade
- Soft color works with many color combinations
- Perfect for patriotic color schemes
- Easy care
- Attracts butterflies

Bloom Color
Pale blue, pink, white, or lavender

Bloom Period
Blooms all summer

Height/Width
5 to 30 inches x 6 to 12 inches

Planting Location
- Well-drained soil but not one that's dry
- Light shade to full sun

Planting
- Plant only after frosts have passed.
- Place plants 6 inches apart.
- Enrich soil with compost or finely shredded bark.

Watering
- After planting, soak deeply.
- Never let ageratum dry out; it likes moist soil.

Fertilizing
- Fertilize twice a month with a water-soluble fertilizer for blooming plants.
- *Or* fertilize twice a season with a pelleted, slow-release fertilizer.

Suggestions for Vigorous Growth
- Regularly pinch off the faded flowers.
- Keep watered and fertilized as directed.

Useful Hint
If blooms brown or fade during hot summer weather, shear them back to produce fresh, pretty new blooms when the temperatures moderate.

Easy Tip
For fuller plants, pinch out the first sets of flowering tips.

- Hose down the plants occasionally, especially in dry weather.

Pest Control
- Watch out for spider mites, which make the leaves turn grayish.
- Spraying the plants with water can prevent or help control spider mites.
- If a chemical control is required for spider mites, look for a miticide because all-purpose insecticides do not affect spider mites.

Complementary Plants
- Use as an edging with white or pink cosmos, yellow marigolds, or coreopsis.
- For a patriotic combination, put white cosmos in the back, red snapdragons in the middle, and blue ageratums in front.

Recommended Selections
- 'Blue Lagoon', which forms a mound about 8 inches high and 8 to 10 inches wide, blooms longer for me than any other ageratum.

Anemone

Anemone × hybrida

A Fall-Blooming Perennial of Delicate Beauty

When you plan a perennial border in which you want something in flower from spring until fall, the most difficult plants to find are the late-season bloomers. Enter anemone. There are three types, one of which is a spring-flowering bulb. But hybrid anemones, often called Japanese anemone, and *Anemone tomentosa* are perennials that bloom in autumn. And unlike most fall-blooming flowers, anemone has delicate blossoms that come in pink, white, or red.

Top Reasons to Plant

- Beautiful, fresh blooms in fall in a springlike color range
- Does well in partial shade
- Insect and disease free
- Spreads quickly in a spot it likes
- Requires little maintenance
- Brightens shade plantings of hostas and ferns
- Flowers sway on long stems in the slightest breeze
- Good cut flower

Useful Hint

Experiment to find the ideal soil for anemones, since they need excellent winter drainage but consistent moisture during the growing season.

Bloom Color
White, rose, and pink

Bloom Period
Late summer and fall

Height/Width
2 to 5 feet x 2 to 3 feet

Planting Location
- Plant in well-drained soil in a naturally moist spot—or water often.
- Partial shade is best.
- Anemone may not do as well in the warmest areas of the state.

Planting
- Plant in early spring or early fall.
- Amend soil with organic matter to add fertility and improve drainage.
- Space plants 1 to 2 feet apart.
- Water thoroughly after planting.
- Mulch well and keep mulch at a 2-inch thickness.

Watering
- Keep soil evenly moist at all times.
- Anemones cannot tolerate drought.
- A site that includes standing water over the winter will kill anemones.

Fertilizing
- Anemone requires little or no fertilizer in good soil.
- Overfertilizing produces fast, floppy growth.

Easy Tip
Anemone is perfect for a shady spot that is always moist in summer.

Suggestions for Vigorous Growth
- Provide anemone the moisture it requires.
- Keep it mulched well to preserve moisture.
- Divide clumps every three years.
- Stake tall stems to avoid damage from thunderstorms.
- Pull up runners if anemones spread too much.

Pest Control
- Anemone has few pest or disease problems.

Complementary Plants
- In partial shade, grow with hostas and ferns to add color.
- Turtlehead (*Chelone* spp.) has similar flower colors and blooms about the same time.

Recommended Selections
- 'Honorine Jobert' is an old cultivar with abundant white flowers filled with contrasting yellow stamens.

Angel Trumpet

Datura wrightii

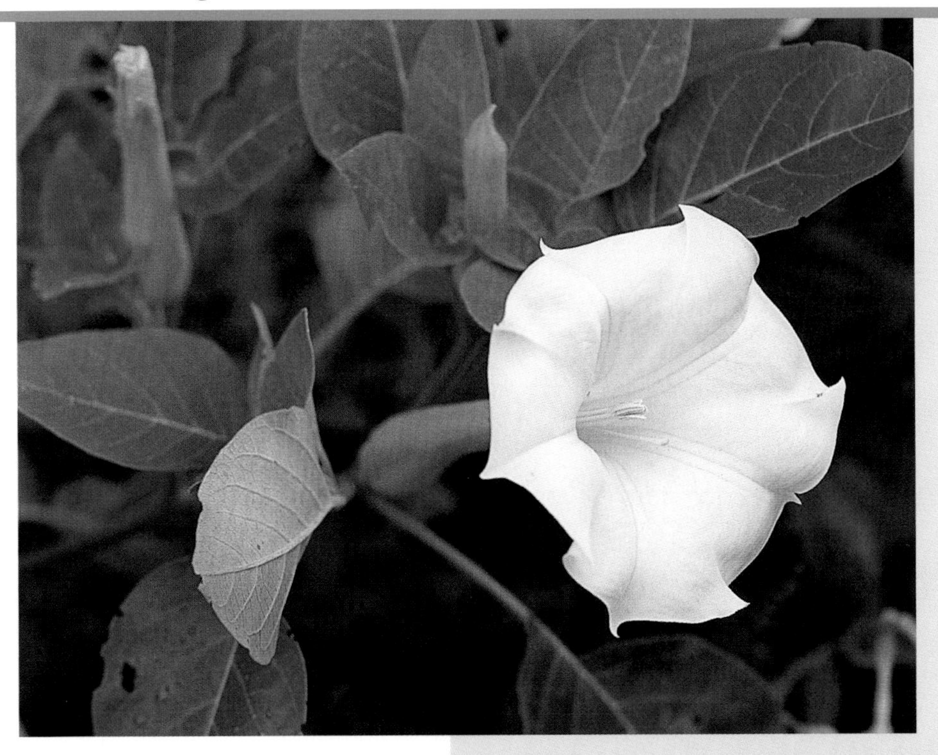

An Exotic Tropical Plant with Showy, Fragrant Blooms

Several different plants are sold as angel trumpet and *Datura*. All are large, lush-growing, tropical plants with bold foliage and beautiful, trumpet-shaped flowers. The first time I saw a group of them in a private garden, it was midsummer, and I felt as if I were in the jungle. If moved into a greenhouse in winter, mature plants may have thirty-five to forty blooms daily. And they're sweetly fragrant.

Top Reasons to Plant

- Lush tropical look
- Large, showy flowers
- Sweet fragrance
- Excellent for containers
- Can overwinter indoors
- Attracts butterflies

Useful Hint

Caution: All parts of the plant, including the seeds and 1½-inch fruit, are very poisonous, so be careful and keep the plant away from young children.

Bloom Color
White, violet

Bloom Period
Summer until fall

Height/Width
3 to 5 feet x 3 to 5 feet

Planting Location
- Soil with plenty of organic matter
- Full sun
- Containers

Planting
- Wait for reliably warm weather (at least May) before planting outdoors.
- Set potted plants outside anytime in summer.

Watering
- Provide plenty of water.
- Keep soil evenly moist.

Fertilizing
- Mix slow-release, pelleted fertilizer with the soil in either the garden or containers.
- *Or* on a regular basis, use water-soluble plant food for flowering plants.

Easy Tip

Cut your datura back and bring it indoors to overwinter with only a little light and very little water.

Suggestions for Vigorous Growth
- Remove faded blooms if they don't drop naturally.
- Overwinter indoors or in a greenhouse.

Pest Control
- Insect and disease problems are few.
- Consult your local Extension Service if pests do appear.

Complementary Plants
- Angel trumpet is usually grown by itself as a specimen plant.
- Try planting a bougainvillea vine in the same tub, letting it scamper up a small trellis.

Recommended Selections
- 'Evening Fragrance' has 8-inch white blooms with a touch of lavender against bluish leaves.

Artemisia

Artemisia 'Powis Castle'

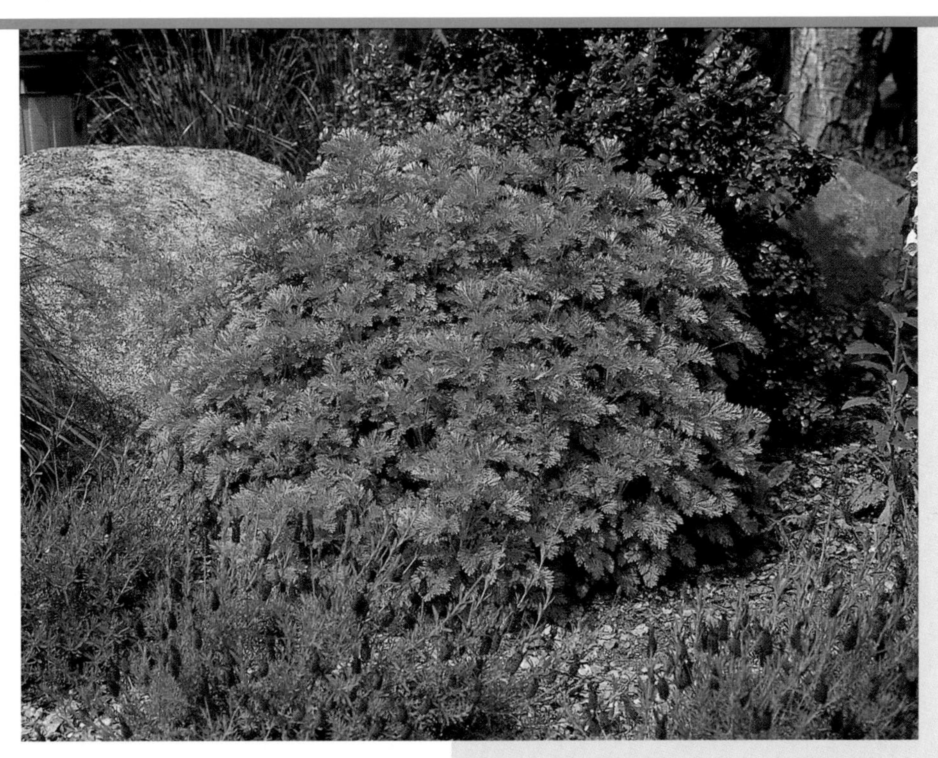

A Perennial with Outstanding, Lacy, Silvery-Gray Foliage

Plants with gray or silver foliage are useful in the garden because of their softening effect and because they complement many flower colors. But gray-leafed plants don't like Tennessee's heat and humidity—they tend to "melt." Artemisia 'Powis Castle' is one that won't melt in the dog days of August, and it also won't take over, as some aggressive types will. It's also drought tolerant and good looking!

Top Reasons to Plant

- Beautiful silvery-gray foliage with fine texture
- Tolerates drought
- Easy care
- Shows off other, more colorful plants
- Softens the look of the garden
- Useful for flower arrangements
- Good filler in the garden

Bloom Color
Grown for lace-cut, silvery-gray leaves

Bloom Period
Foliage effective from summer to fall

Height/Width
3 feet x 3 feet

Planting Location
- Well-drained soil
- Full sun, but stands a little afternoon shade

Planting
- Set out purchased plants or rooted cuttings in spring.
- Add organic matter to the soil to ensure good drainage.
- Water well after planting.
- Do not mulch.

Watering
- Once established, 'Powis Castle' shouldn't need watering.

Fertilizing
- No fertilizer is required.

Suggestions for Vigorous Growth
- Prune 'Powis Castle' in spring, as needed.
- If plants flop over in summer, cut them back to 2 inches tall.

Useful Hint

Produce more plants by rooting the cuttings you pinch off in a mixture of 1 part sand to 1 part potting soil.

Easy Tip

If artemisia spreads farther than you like, cut off some of the plants and use them in flower arrangements indoors.

- Pinch the growing tips of the plant throughout the season to keep 'Powis Castle' compact.
- Do not overwater.

Pest Control
- Yellow spots on the lower leaves indicates rust, a fungal disease that can develop in humid conditions.
- If rust develops, cut the plant back to the ground, removing all leaves from the garden and destroying them.

Complementary Plants
- 'Powis Castle' is an excellent filler plant with antique or English roses, asters, purple coneflowers, other perennials, and flowering shrubs.

Recommended Selections
- Another artemisia that tends not to melt in our climate is *Artemisia schmidtiana* 'Silverado', which has a lower, mounding form.

Baptisia

Baptisia species and hybrids

A Native Perennial with Graceful Blue or White Flower Stalks

Baptisia is a plant with a past. Native to the United States, it was used in the 1700s as a substitute for indigo, which wouldn't grow here, to make dye for cloth. Its common name is false indigo. Gardeners enjoy two types—*Baptisia australis* (sometimes called blue false indigo) and *Baptisia alba* (white false indigo). Both produce stalks of pealike blooms. The two make a fine combination.

Top Reasons to Plant

- Beautiful spring flowers
- Easy-care native plant
- Drought tolerant when established
- Attractive seedpods
- Beautiful bluish green foliage attractive after blooms fade
- Long spring-blooming season
- Attractive to butterflies and hummingbirds
- Interesting history

Bloom Color
Blue or white

Bloom Period
Spring

Height/Width
3 to 4 feet x 4 to 5 feet

Planting Location
- Prefers rich, organic soil that drains well, but tolerates average soil.
- Blue type needs full sun.
- White type does nicely in partial shade or sun.

Planting
- Set out plants in spring.
- *Or* sow fresh seed in late summer.
- Space plants 3 feet apart; once established, baptisia is difficult to move successfully.
- Water well after planting.
- Mulch to keep soil cool.

Watering
- Water regularly to avoid wilting during the first year; after that, baptisia tolerates drought.

Fertilizing
- Spread pelleted, slow-release fertilizer over the soil in spring.
- If leaves yellow prematurely during summer, use a water-soluble fertilizer for flowering plants that contains iron.

Useful Hint
White false indigo is shorter than blue false indigo, and it blooms a few weeks later.

Easy Tip
Leave the last round of flowers on the plant to form attractive seedpods that sway in the wind.

Suggestions for Vigorous Growth
- Young plants, or those in partial shade, may need staking.
- Cut off faded flowers to promote continuing bloom.
- Baptisia is slow to begin blooming, usually showing a few blooms the second year but many more in the third—fertilize in spring to encourage faster growth.
- Seed-grown plants may take up to five years to reach their full glory, so fertilize in spring to speed them along.

Pest Control
- Voles may be a problem, but otherwise baptisia is generally very healthy.

Complementary Plants
- Bearded iris, peonies, Shasta daisies, black-eyed Susans, and cleome are good companions.

Recommended Selections
- *Baptisia alba* 'Pendula' has a slightly weeping habit and white flowers.
- *Baptisia* 'Purple Smoke' has lavender-gray flowers.

Black-Eyed Susan

Rudbeckia species and hybrids

A Perennial Bright Blooming Machine from Summer to Fall

Black-eyed Susan warms up any bed with its golden yellow-orange flowers. The one most often found in nurseries is *Rudbeckia* 'Goldsturm', which grows about 2 feet high and is a blooming machine from summer until fall, if you remove faded flowers. Be careful when you buy plants, since some *Rudbeckia*, such as the impressive hybrids of *Rudbeckia hirta*, are annuals. 'Goldsturm' is the best all-around choice.

Top Reasons to Plant

- Bright blossoms for many weeks
- Insect and disease free
- Easy to grow
- Drought tolerant when established
- Seedheads attract birds
- Good cut flower
- Low maintenance
- Spreads quickly
- Tolerates some shade

Useful Hint

Some *Rudbeckia* species, usually called coneflowers, may reach 5 to 7 feet tall and are very impressive—if you have room for them.

Bloom Color
Gold and yellow

Bloom Period
Summer to fall

Height/Width
8 inches to 3 feet x 18 inches

Planting Location
- Well-drained soil
- Full or partial sun

Planting
- Space *Rudbeckia fulgida* species and 'Goldsturm' 18 inches apart.
- Space cutleaf coneflower (*Rudbeckia laciniata*) 1 foot apart.
- Space *Rudbeckia nitida* 2 feet apart.
- Water well after planting.
- Mulch lightly.

Watering
- Water frequently to keep root zone moist until plants are established.
- Mature plants tolerate drought.

Fertilizing
- No fertilizer is needed except in very poor soil.
- If fertilizer is needed, spread a pelleted, slow-release type in early spring.
- *Or* use a water-soluble flower fertilizer monthly during the growing season.

Easy Tip
Dig up the offsets and self-seeded plants, pot them, and give them away as gifts.

Suggestions for Vigorous Growth
- Remove spent flowers to prolong bloom.
- Divide black-eyed Susan every three years in spring or early fall.
- Lift and replant offsets and new seedlings any time during the growing season.

Pest Control
- Spider mites may occur in very dry sites in midsummer; spray with water weekly to prevent them.
- Mildew may appear in late fall but is not a problem.

Complementary Plants
- Butterfly weed, red-leafed coleus, and ornamental grasses make good neighbors.

Recommended Selections
- 'Goldsturm' is one flower that should be in every garden.

Bleeding Heart

Dicentra spectabilis

A Shade Loving Perennial with Showy Dangling Heart-Shaped Flowers

Take dangling, heart-shaped flowers, arch them over deeply cut leaves in shades of green, gray, and blue, and the lovely result is bleeding heart. If you have a shade garden, overlook the gory name and grow this plant; it's a must for every yard in spring. You'll find several choices of species—I especially like the fernlike leaves of fringed bleeding heart (*Dicentra eximia*), a native plant.

Top Reasons to Plant

- Showy spring flowers
- Loves shade
- Attractive foliage
- Unusual cut flower
- Attracts butterflies and hummingbirds
- Old-fashioned, native plant
- Excellent in woodland garden

Bloom Color
Pink, red, or white

Bloom Period
Late spring, or sometimes summer and early fall

Height/Width
8 to 24 inches x 12 to 18 inches

Planting Location
- Rich soil that drains quickly but doesn't dry out between waterings
- Shade or partial shade

Planting
- Add organic matter to soil to improve its fertility and drainage.
- Plant dormant roots or purchased plants in spring.
- Space plants or roots 18 inches to 2 feet apart.
- Water thoroughly after planting.
- Mulch lightly.

Watering
- Water deeply in spring if rainfall is less than normal.
- If plants wilt in spring, water more often and add mulch.

Fertilizing
- Fertilize with a balanced, slow-release, pelleted fertilizer when leaves appear every year.

Useful Hint

Look for the new hybrids of bleeding heart, many of which bloom into summer and fall.

Easy Tip

When bleeding heart goes dormant in summer, plant shade-loving annuals around it to fill the empty space.

Suggestions for Vigorous Growth
- Expect the plant to go dormant (leaves yellow and disappear) by early summer.
- Pull up plants that result from self-sown seeds—their flowers won't look like the parent plant.
- Divide crowded clumps in spring or fall by cutting pieces of the rhizome into pieces with two to four buds each.
- Do not divide unless plants are truly overcrowded; it takes several years for plants to recover.

Pest Control
- There are few pests or diseases.

Complementary Plants
- This makes an excellent woodland plant with ferns, hostas, and foamflower (*Tiarella*).
- Hide the dormant bleeding heart with clumps of annual, rose-colored impatiens.

Recommended Selections
- 'Pantaloons' has pure-white blossoms that combine nicely with many more brightly colored spring flowers.
- 'Luxuriant' has fire-engine red blooms and blue-green foliage.

Butterfly Weed

Asclepias tuberosa

A Perennial Native Plant Beloved by Butterflies

As its name implies, butterfly weed attracts the "winged jewels" by the dozen, especially the beautiful monarch butterflies. (It also provides nectar for moths at night.) But I'd grow this attractive native plant even if it didn't. I love the bright-orange flower clusters sitting atop shiny green leaves. And it couldn't be simpler to grow. As long as it's in the sun, it's carefree.

Top Reasons to Plant

- Attracts butterflies
- Beautiful, showy blooms
- Easy care
- Drought tolerant when established

Useful Hint

New hybrids of butterfly weed feature red or yellow blooms, but in Tennessee, orange is likely to top the popularity poll for years to come.

Bloom Color
Orange, red, pink, yellow, or white

Bloom Period
Summer

Height/Width
2 to 3 feet x 2 feet

Planting Location
- Average, well-drained soil; too much moisture, especially in winter, and the plant won't return the next spring
- Full sun—too little causes the plant to flop over
- Choose location with care; this plant's deep taproot usually breaks apart fatally when transplanting.

Planting
- Plant in early spring.
- Space plants 10 to 12 inches apart.
- Plant carefully to avoid breaking the taproot.
- Use a liquid root stimulator when planting.

Watering
- Established plants rarely need extra water.

Fertilizing
- No fertilizer is required unless plants are not growing well.

Suggestions for Vigorous Growth
- Remove faded flowers to encourage a longer blooming time.
- Leave the second wave of flowers on the stems so the purple pods, which are great in flower arrangements, will open in late fall.

Easy Tip
Don't worry if you see caterpillars munching butterfly weed—they'll likely turn into beautiful monarch butterflies.

- Instead of dividing clumps, cut back plants to rejuvenate them.

Pest Control
- Few pests are a problem except aphids, which can be dislodged with a spray of water from the garden hose or treated with insecticidal soap.
- Caterpillars found munching on butterfly weed are the larvae of the monarch butterfly, so don't kill them.
- If caterpillars do too much damage, try transferring them onto butterfly weed or milkweed growing in the wild.

Complementary Plants
- Use in a wildflower meadow.
- Pair with Shasta daisy, black-eyed Susan, and red hot poker. Combine orange types with *Achillea* 'Moonshine' and pale-yellow Asiatic lilies.

Recommended Selections
- 'Hello Yellow' has flowers exactly the color you would expect.
- A butterfly weed relative, *Asclepias incarnata*, is ideal for always-damp spots in the yard or garden.

Cardinal Flower

Lobelia cardinalis

A Gorgeous Late-Summer-Blooming Perennial Beloved by Hummingbirds

The list of cardinal flower's attributes makes it sound too good to be true. It grows in partial shade or shade, blooms in late summer when few other perennials do, produces tall spikes of brilliant red flowers much loved by hummingbirds, and self-sows so you always have a group of cardinal flowers. As if that weren't enough, it also stays in flower at least three weeks.

Top Reasons to Plant

- Hummingbirds love it
- Thrives in shade or partial shade
- Ideal for that always-damp spot in your yard
- Blooms in late summer when few other perennials do
- Has tall spikes of brilliant red flowers
- Self-seeds readily
- Needs little care in the moist situation it prefers

Useful Hint

Plant cardinal flower in a shady corner near the house to bring hummingbirds into viewing range from a window.

Bloom Color
Red or pink

Bloom Period
Late summer

Height/Width
2 to 4 feet x 2 feet

Planting Location
- Rich, organic soil amended with compost or other material so it retains moisture
- Partial sun or shade

Planting
- Set plants out in spring.
- Space them 18 to 24 inches apart.
- Mix pelleted, slow-release fertilizer into the planting hole.
- Water well after planting.
- Mulch well.

Watering
- Cardinal flower needs consistently moist soil, so watering enough is the key to success.
- Install a soaker hose to keep cardinal flower gently watered if it's in dry soil.

Fertilizing
- If a slow-release fertilizer was incorporated at planting, additional fertilizer usually isn't needed.
- If lower leaves turn yellow, spray with a water-soluble fertilizer made for flowering plants that contains iron.

Easy Tip
Cardinal flower is a great choice for that shady, soggy spot in your yard.

Suggestions for Vigorous Growth
- Pruning, pinching, and dividing are seldom needed.
- Pull back the mulch around this often short-lived plant after bloom to enable self-seeding.

Pest Control
- In the moist soil it loves, cardinal flower has few insects or diseases.
- If cardinal flower is growing in a dry area, aphids and spider mites may be a problem.
- Ask the Extension Service about controls, and water more often.

Complementary Plants
- Plant with flag iris near a water garden.

Recommended Selections
- 'Rose Beacon' has rosy-pink flowers on 40-inch stems.
- 'Shrimp Salad' is an unusual color for cardinal flowers—a soft, shrimp pink.

Celosia

Celosia argentea Plumosa group

An Outrageously Showy Annual for Lovers of Bright Colors

Celosia isn't for the faint of heart. Not because it's difficult to grow, but because of the spiky, fire-engine red flowers that, when planted *en masse*, look as though a fire has started. Yellow, orange, and pink hybrids are also available, but red seems to be the color of choice, even in the old-fashioned cockscomb (*Celosia argentea* Cristata group), which produces velvety, convoluted blooms resembling a rooster's comb.

Top Reasons to Plant

- Tolerates heat and drought
- Bright blooms in unusual shapes
- Good for drying
- Adds strong vertical accent

Useful Hint

Celosia tolerates both heat and drought, asking no more of a gardener than to remove faded flowers.

Bloom Color
Red, yellow, orange, or pink

Bloom Period
Summer to frost

Height/Width
8 inches to 3 feet x 8 to 12 inches

Planting Location
- Fertile soil holds moisture, although it tolerates average, well-drained soil
- Full sun or light afternoon shade

Planting
- If growing from seed started indoors, sow seed about eight weeks before you plan to transplant outside.
- If growing from seed started outdoors, sow seed two weeks after the average last frost date.
- Set out nursery plants and indoor seedlings after the soil has warmed.
- Space plants 9 to 12 inches apart.
- Mix pelleted, slow-release fertilizer into the planting hole.
- Water well after planting.

Watering
- Water often enough that young plants do not dry out.
- After plants are established, watering only in dry spells should be enough.

Fertilizing
- Fertilize twice a month with a liquid plant food for flowering plants.

Easy Tip

Try cutting some of the fully open flowers, hanging them upside down in a warm, dry place indoors, and drying them for winter arrangements.

Suggestions for Vigorous Growth
- Pinch the stems back for a bushier plant—but a bushier plant is heavier and often needs staking to avoid thunderstorm damage.
- Remove flowers as they fade.

Pest Control
- Celosia has few pests, but if a plant turns completely yellow, it's diseased; remove it from the bed and destroy it.

Complementary Plants
- Plant white petunias in front of red-flowered celosia.
- Plant red-flowered celosia in front of white morning glories.

Recommended Selections
- *Celosia argentea* 'Prestige Scarlet' produces multiple branches.
- *Celosia argentea* 'Apricot Brandy' has gold blooms against green-purple foliage.

Chrysanthemum

Dendranthema × grandiflora

A Favorite Colorful Perennial Bloomer That Says "Fall"

It simply wouldn't feel like fall without colorful chrysanthemums. Most of us buy them already in bloom. Or hating to throw away gift plants, we place pots of florists' mums in the garden once the weather warms up. But it's also enjoyable to buy mums as small plants in spring, and grow them to blooming size in fall. There's a nice feeling of satisfaction from doing it yourself.

Top Reasons to Plant

- Bright flowers late in the season
- Wide variety of bloom shapes and colors
- Showy when planted in a mass
- Good for fall containers
- Combines well with other fall bloomers
- It wouldn't be fall without them!

Useful Hint

Pinching mums back causes the plant to form a more compact shape and be less likely to require staking.

Bloom Color
White, yellow, pink, and shades of red, orange, and purple

Bloom Period
Fall

Height/Width
10 to 48 inches x 10 to 30 inches

Planting Location
- Well-drained soil amended with organic matter
- Full sun

Planting
- Plant florists' mums outdoors anytime the weather is frost free.
- Set out bedding plants in spring.
- Water with a transplanting solution.
- Mix pelleted, slow-release fertilizer with the soil.
- Mulch heavily, as mums have shallow roots.

Watering
- Water regularly to ensure the soil doesn't dry out.

Fertilizing
- Fertilize starting in June, using a water-soluble fertilizer for flowering plants every other week until buds form.
- After buds form, stop fertilizing.

Easy Tip
Avoid planting mums in spots with dusk-to-dawn lighting—they won't bloom without nighttime darkness.

Suggestions for Vigorous Growth
- From late spring to July 15, occasionally pinch 2 inches off the tips of the stems; if you don't, they'll bloom in summer, not fall.
- After plants are killed by frost, wait until spring to cut them back.
- Every other spring, dig up and divide the plant, discarding the woody center portion.

Pest Control
- If aphids or spider mites appear, ask the Extension Service about a control.

Complementary Plants
- Plant with other fall bloomers, such as asters.
- Use in mass groupings where annuals might otherwise be used, such as between the sidewalk and driveway or street.

Recommended Selections
- *Dendranthema zawadskii*, (*Chrysanthemum rubellum*) 'Clara Curtis' is easy to grow and has deep-pink, daisylike blooms on 2-foot plants.

Cleome

Cleome hassleriana

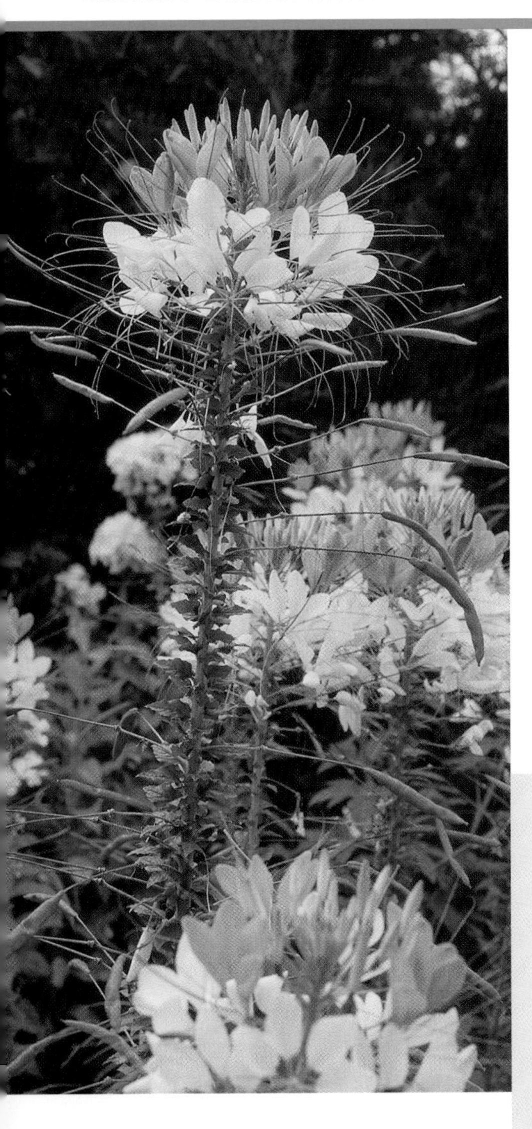

A Lovely Old-Fashioned Annual That Beats the Heat

If your grandmother or great-grandmother was a gardener, she grew cleome. But later, people wanted to buy bedding plants, not grow flowers from seed, and they wanted short plants, not tall ones. So lovely cleome, also called spider flower, fell out of favor. But now it's back. And a good thing it is, too. In Chinese, the common name of cleome is drunk butterflies. Look closely at the airy blooms, and you'll see why.

Top Reasons to Plant

- Tall, graceful blooms
- Unusual flower shape
- Withstands heat and humidity
- Self-seeds readily
- Easy to grow
- Has few pests or diseases
- Fragrant
- Attracts butterflies and hummingbirds

Useful Hint

In midsummer, when the yard looks tired, cleome shines, completely unaffected by the heat.

Bloom Color
Pink, rose, purple, or white

Bloom Period
Midsummer until frost

Height/Width
3 to 6 feet x 1 to 1½ feet

Planting Location
- Average, well-drained soil
- Full sun to light afternoon shade
- Out of the wind

Planting
- Refrigerate cleome seeds during winter, then plant after the last expected frost.
- *Or* sow seeds indoors in a warm environment six to eight weeks before the last expected frost.
- Thin or set plants 18 to 24 inches apart.
- Use a liquid root stimulator, and mix a pelleted, slow-release fertilizer into the soil.
- Water plants well.
- Mulch very lightly or not at all to permit cleome to reseed.

Watering
- Water often enough to prevent wilting; once dried out, cleome may not grow or bloom well.

Fertilizing
- Fertilize weekly with a water-soluble plant food, such as 20-20-20.

Easy Tip
Let some of the flowers set seeds and self-sow—you'll never be without cleome.

Suggestions for Vigorous Growth
- When plants are a foot tall, pinch an inch off the tip of the main stem to encourage branching.
- Mulch lightly to permit cleome to reseed itself.

Pest Control
- If aphids appear, spray with insecticidal soap.
- If leaf spot develops, pick off the affected leaves and dispose of them.

Complementary Plants
- Plant a group of cleomes at the back of a flower bed with tall annuals, such as standard zinnias, in front to mask cleome's leggy stems.
- For a nice look, plant cleome with silver-leafed artemisia at its base.

Recommended Selections
- 'Helen Campbell', which grows about 4 feet tall, has glossy white flowers.
- 'Cherry Queen' is a pretty rose color.

Coleus

Solenostemon scutellarioides

A "Newly Trendy" Old-Fashioned Annual with Gorgeous Foliage

Who would've imagined old-fashioned coleus as a trendy plant? But in the past few years, that's just what it has become. Plant breeders have developed hybrids with leaves in brilliant color combinations that will knock your socks off. And most of these new cultivars—propagated from cuttings instead of seeds—don't bloom, saving you the chore of pinching off the flower spikes. Many also tolerate a fair amount of sun.

Top Reasons to Plant

- Beautiful foliage in brilliant color combinations
- Excellent in containers or in the garden
- Tolerates sun or shade
- Usually pest and disease free
- Combines well with other annuals and with perennials
- Easy to grow
- Roots readily from cuttings to produce more plants

Useful Hint

When it comes to versatile plants that can take the heat, coleus comes through with shining colors.

Bloom Color
Foliage in shades of red, pink, gold, chartreuse, and bicolors

Bloom Period
Foliage effective from spring until frost

Height/Width
6 inches to 4 feet x 8 inches to 3 feet

Planting Location
- Moist, well-drained soil amended with organic matter to improve drainage
- Some tolerate more sun than others, so check the plant label to see whether it's a sun or shade coleus.
- Leaf colors are usually more intense in shade or partial shade.

Planting
- Set out plants after all chance of spring frost has passed.
- Space plants 6 to 18 inches apart, depending on mature size.
- Mix pelleted, slow-release fertilizer with the soil in the planting hole.
- Water well and mulch heavily.

Watering
- Water regularly to prevent drying out.
- Be especially careful to water plants in containers and hanging baskets.

Fertilizing
- Feed once a month with a water-soluble fertilizer, such as 20-20-20.

Suggestions for Vigorous Growth
- Lightly pinch the tips of the stems of upright coleus when they are 4 to 6 inches tall to encourage branching.
- Continue pinching occasionally as needed to prevent a leggy appearance.
- Pick off flowers as they appear; once they open, plants begin to decline.

Easy Tip
Root cuttings of coleus in water, then plant the cuttings in pots for a sunny window indoors over the winter.

Pest Control
- Watch for snails and slugs; if they appear, ask at a garden center about new organic controls for them.

Complementary Plants
- Grow red coleus with silver-leafed dusty miller and other colors of coleus with perennial flowers or geraniums of the same shade.
- Gold and chartreuse coleus look nice with yellow and green hostas.

Recommended Selections
- 'Trailing Red', which has small leaves and red stems, works well in containers.
- 'Bellingrath Pink' is red when grown in the sun and chartreuse in the shade.

Columbine

Aquilegia species and hybrids

A Graceful, Colorful Perennial That Shouts "Spring Is Here!"

I can't imagine a wildflower garden without columbine in it. Almost everyone knows the plant because of the distinctive—often two-toned—nodding flowers and fan-shaped leaves that are columbine's trademarks. They're a must for attracting hummingbirds and butterflies, but most of all for their sheer beauty. If you haven't seen columbine lately, you'll be surprised at the new flower colors and variegated leaves.

Top Reasons to Plant

- Beautiful two-toned flowers
- Flowers with unusual shape
- Attracts butterflies and hummingbirds
- Mixes well with both spring wildflowers and border plants
- Grows nicely in partial shade
- Reseeds readily

Useful Hint

Plant columbines at the front of a border or along a path where their delicate nature can be appreciated.

Bloom Color
Red, yellow, white, blue, purple, or pink

Bloom Period
Spring

Height/Width
9 inches to 3 feet x 1 foot

Planting Location
- Rich organic soil that holds moisture but drains rapidly
- Sun or partial shade

Planting
- Set out anytime during the growing season, but mid-spring is best.
- Space plants about 1 foot apart.
- Water well after planting.
- Mulch to cool soil and hold moisture but do not bury the crown of the plant.

Watering
- Water as needed so soil stays just moist.
- Do not permit to dry out.

Fertilizing
- Columbine doesn't usually need fertilizer—the mulch breaks down, gently feeding the plant.

Suggestions for Vigorous Growth
- Columbine rarely lives more than a few years but reseeds itself.
- To avoid reseeding, remove flowers as they fade.
- *Or* deadhead the first flowers to encourage more blooms, then allow the second blooms to set seed.

Easy Tip
Let the last wave of flowers set seeds; pull back the mulch around the plants so you'll have a new supply of plants next spring.

Pest Control
- Columbine is subject to attacks by a large number of insects, from caterpillars (which devour leaves) to leaf miners (which leave little "trails" in the foliage).
- Check with the Extension Service about controls.

Complementary Plants
- Combine columbines with perennials that flower later in the year, such as asters in sun or ferns and hostas in shade.
- Use with Siberian iris and other spring bloomers.

Recommended Selections
- 'Crimson Star' has eye-catching red and white blooms.
- 'Lime Frost' has beautiful yellow and green variegated leaves on a plant that grows 18 to 20 inches tall.

Coreopsis

Coreopsis grandiflora

A Showy Sunshine-Yellow Perennial That Stops Traffic

One spring I dug up all the shrubs along my front walkway and planted perennials instead. Into one section went six *Coreopsis grandiflora* plants. Two years later, thanks to the plant's habit of reseeding, I had a row 6 feet long and 3 feet wide. In mid-May, it became a sea of sunshiny yellow, putting on such a show that strangers would stop and ask what that plant was.

Useful Hint

Although it isn't as showy, threadleaf coreopsis (*Coreopsis verticillata* 'Moonbeam') has creamy-yellow flowers that look beautiful with pastel-pink or blue blossoms.

Top Reasons to Plant

- Bright yellow flowers
- Reseeds easily
- Low maintenance
- Good cut flower
- Attracts butterflies
- Drought tolerant when established
- Few insect or disease problems
- Seedheads attract goldfinches

Bloom Color
Bright yellow to gold

Bloom Period
May to June

Height/Width
1 to 3 feet x 6 to 18 inches

Planting Location
- Average, well-drained soil
- Full sun

Planting
- Set out plants in spring after danger of frost has passed.
- Plant anytime up to September.
- Place plants 12 to 18 inches apart.
- Water well after planting.

Watering
- Water regularly while plants are young.
- Mature plants generally tolerate drought.

Fertilizing
- No fertilizer is needed.

Suggestions for Vigorous Growth
- Stake taller cultivars to prevent thunderstorm damage.
- Remove faded flowers to encourage reblooming and to prevent reseeding.
- Deadhead with pruners as pinching off old flowers by hand is time consuming.
- Allow to set seed, and plants will spread by reseeding.
- Divide plants every three years.

Easy Tip

Coreopsis seedpods attract goldfinches, which entertain us by standing on their heads to reach into the seedpods.

Pest Control
- If aphids appear, knock them off with a stream of water or spray with insecticidal soap.

Complementary Plants
- Mass coreopsis plants for an excellent effect.
- Combine with Shasta daisy 'Becky' and goldenrod.

Recommended Selections
- 'Early Sunrise' stays under 2 feet tall and blooms the longest.
- 'Zagreb' is charming at the front of a border.

Cosmos

Cosmos bipinnatus

A Cheerful Annual Anyone Can Grow

Cosmos has ferny foliage and airy single flowers with yellow disks in the center—much like daisies but more delicate. Despite its appearance, you don't have to treat cosmos with kid gloves. It thrives in poor soil, rarely needs water once it has developed a good root system, and almost never requires fertilizer. The reward for this neglect is armloads of blooms in your garden and full vases from summer to frost.

Top Reasons to Plant

- Easy, easy, easy
- Heavy bloomer
- Good cut flower
- Reseeds readily
- Essential for both cottage gardens and natural landscapes
- Drought resistant when established
- Few pests and diseases

Useful Hint

Cosmos is so easy to grow that many highway departments use it along roadways.

Bloom Color
White, pink, rose, and fuchsia

Bloom Period
Midsummer to frost

Height/Width
2 to 6 feet x 1 to 2½ feet

Planting Location
- Well-drained, poor to average soil
- Full sun
- Protection from wind

Planting
- Start seeds indoors six weeks before the last expected frost.
- Sow seeds in single pots rather than flats to avoid disturbing the roots.
- *Or* sow seeds outdoors in a sunny spot and let them grow.
- Space homegrown or nursery plants 12 to 18 inches apart.
- Water with a root stimulator after planting.
- Mulch lightly or not at all to encourage reseeding.

Watering
- Water regularly until plants become established.
- Mature plants need little watering, but soak the soil well each time you do water.

Fertilizing
- Fertilize sparingly.
- Apply a water-soluble plant food for flowers once—at midsummer.
- Avoid overfertilizing; too much fertilizer or overrich soil causes weak stems.

Easy Tip
Avoid windy sites for tall cosmos or you'll have to stake them.

Suggestions for Vigorous Growth
- Pinch back tall varieties when they are 12 to 18 inches tall for maximum flowers.
- Snip off faded blooms to keep the flowers coming.

Pest Control
- If aphids are a problem, spray them with insecticidal soap or a blast of water.

Complementary Plants
- Use shorter varieties at the front of a bed or border.
- Place taller types at the rear of a bed or border to add a vertical accent.

Recommended Selections
- Brightly colored 'Imperial Pink' grows 4 feet tall.
- Available in yellow, orange, and red selections, *Cosmos sulphureus* has sturdy stems and blooms earlier in the season than *Cosmos bipinnatus*.

Daylily

Hemerocallis hybrids

A Versatile Perennial with Carefree Color

There's much more to daylilies than the gangly orange ones that bloom along roadsides or 'Stella d'Oro'. Stella has the wonderful trait of blooming several times over the season, but don't stop with it. You'll find daylilies with spidery flowers in colors that appear to be dusted with gold or silver and with the curved and ruffled blossoms that I love. Today's daylilies are really something to look at—and they're still carefree.

Top Reasons to Plant

- Easy to grow
- Wide range of bright colors
- Drought tolerant when established
- Few insects or diseases
- Increases rapidly and can be divided to produce more plants
- Straplike foliage attractive even after bloom

Useful Hint

Plant daylilies with daffodils so the growing daylilies help hide the dying daffodil foliage.

Bloom Color
Every color except true blue and true white

Bloom Period
Late spring to fall

Height/Width
6 inches to 6 feet x 18 inches to 3 feet

Planting Location
- Will survive in almost any soil, but for best growth, amend soil with organic matter
- Partial to full sun

Planting
- Plant tuberous roots in spring after frosts have passed.
- Set out purchased plants anytime from spring to late summer.
- Space plants 1 to 2 feet apart.
- Add a pelleted, slow-release fertilizer to the planting hole.
- Water well after planting.

Watering
- Keep new plantings moist until new growth appears.
- Then water when rainfall is below normal.
- Give rebloomers an inch of water weekly from the end of their first flowering period until new buds form.

Fertilizing
- Fertilize with a slow-release plant food each spring after leaves appear.
- *Or* use a water-soluble fertilizer for flowering plants every other week during the growing season.

Easy Tip

If you're gardening on a budget, buy just a few daylilies and then divide the clumps every few years.

Suggestions for Vigorous Growth
- Faithfully pick off faded flowers.
- Do not allow seedpods to form.
- Cut down the stalks completely after flowering.
- Allow the leaves to stand until killed by a freeze.
- Divide crowded clumps in spring.

Pest Control
- Daylilies generally have few pests or diseases, but rust has become troublesome in the South—ask the Extension Service for advice.

Complementary Plants
- Enjoy daylilies massed on their own.
- Use with other perennials and annuals in complementary colors.

Recommended Selections
- 'Happy Returns' is a good repeat bloomer in a soft yellow that many prefer to 'Stella d'Oro'.
- 'Winning Ways', an old favorite in a beautiful yellow, never fails to look wonderful, no matter the weather.

Dianthus

Dianthus species and hybrids

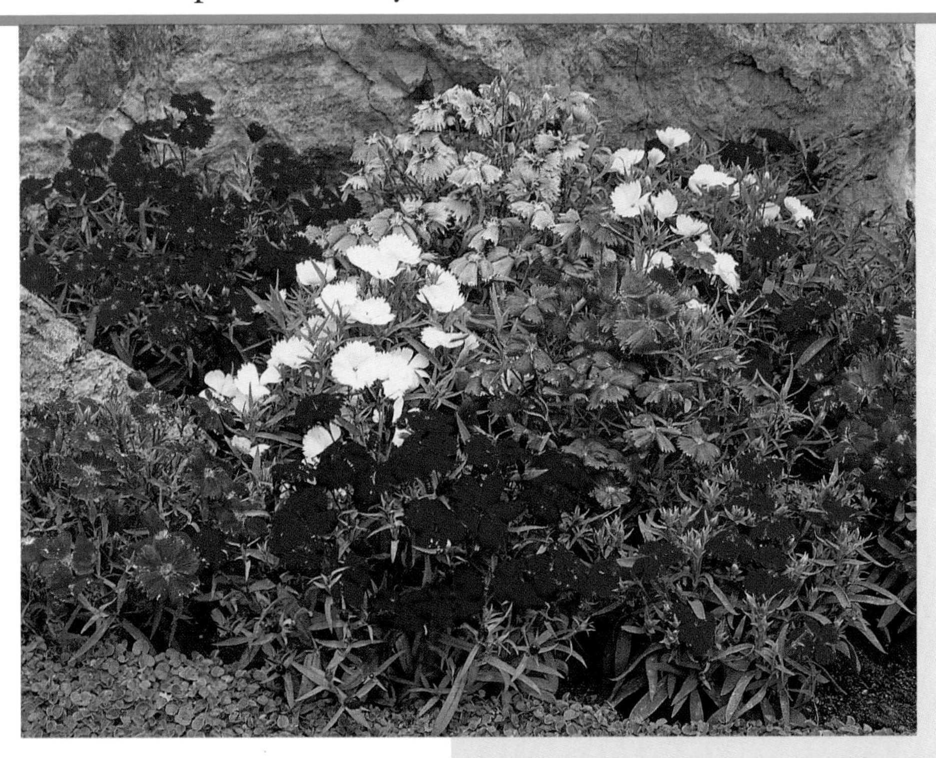

An Old-Fashioned Perennial with Spicy Fragrance

The old-fashioned name for this group of plants is "pinks"—Allwood pinks (*Dianthus Alwoodii*), cheddar pinks (*D. gratianopolitanus*), cottage pinks (*D. plumarius*), and maiden pinks (*D. deltoides*). Even sweet William (*D. barbatus*) can be considered part of the family. All have spicily fragrant flowers that are long-lasting in a vase. The foliage may be green or gray. There are so many to choose from, you're sure to want several.

Top Reasons to Plant

- Bright flowers
- Spicy fragrance
- Old-fashioned look
- Generally pest free
- Good cut flower
- Attractive foliage after bloom

Useful Hint

Dianthus is the perfect plant for a cottage garden look.

Bloom Color
Pink, white, or red

Bloom Period
Late spring to early summer

Height/Width
2 inches to 2 feet x 1 to 2 feet

Planting Location
- Well-drained, slightly alkaline soil
- Naturally acidic soil needs lime added in fall before spring planting.
- Full sun

Planting
- Set out plants in spring.
- Space sweet William types 10 to 12 inches apart.
- Plant mat-forming pinks at least 15 inches apart.
- Water well after planting.
- Mulch the sweet William types but not the ground huggers.

Watering
- Avoid overwatering; it leads to leaf diseases.
- Provide additional water during droughts.

Fertilizing
- If soil is poor, fertilize in spring, before buds form, with a water-soluble fertilizer made for flowers.
- Fertilize sweet William types monthly.

Easy Tip
Spreading types of pinks look great at the front of a border or in a rock garden.

Suggestions for Vigorous Growth
- Deadhead faithfully to promote reblooming and to keep plants looking neat.
- Cut sweet William stalks to the ground after flowering.
- Shear mat-forming pinks after flowering.
- Divide plants every three years or so.

Pest Control
- Few pests bother dianthus, but sweet William attracts rabbits.

Complementary Plants
- Combine low-growing types with candytuft and tulips or with heuchera.

Recommended Selections
- 'Laced Hero' features patterned burgundy and white blooms.
- 'Bath's Pink' is considered the best southern performer.

Foxglove

Digitalis species and hybrids

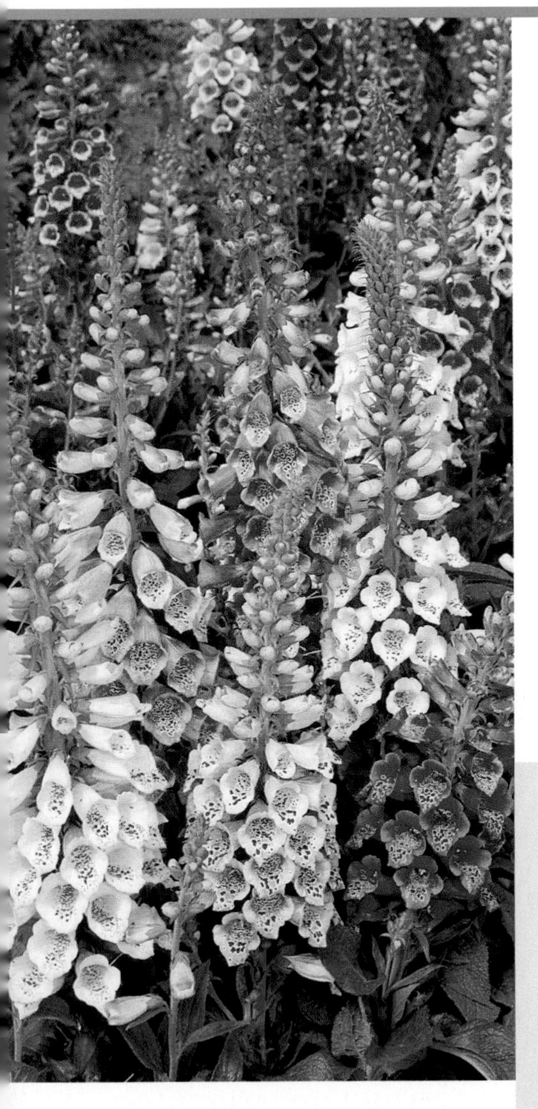

A Romantic Plant with Elegant Spires of Flowers

Foxglove's stately spires of tubular blooms are both beautiful and romantic. But when gardeners hunt for plants, they often get confused. Some foxgloves are grown as annuals, and the most common kind (*Digitalis purpurea*) is a biennial, which grows one year, then flowers and dies the next. But there are also truly perennial foxgloves, such as *Digitalis grandiflora* and *Digitalis* × *mertonensis*.

Top Reasons to Plant

- Stately, beautiful flower spikes
- Blooms in wide range of colors
- Excellent in moist, woodland settings
- Gives romantic, old-fashioned feel to garden
- Good cut flower
- Strong vertical accent
- Takes some shade
- Few pests
- Attracts butterflies and hummingbirds

Useful Hint

Whichever type of foxglove you choose, plant it in the right conditions and you'll have plants forever since all foxgloves reseed prolifically.

Bloom Color
Lavender, yellow, pink, white, strawberry-red, or purple

Bloom Period
Spring and summer

Height/Width
2 to 5 feet x 18 inches

Planting Location
- Moist soil rich in organic matter
- Partial shade

Planting
- Set out plants in early spring.
- If growing from seed, start seeds in summer and transplant seedlings in early fall.
- Space plants 12 inches apart.
- Add a pelleted, slow-release fertilizer to the planting hole.
- Water well after planting.
- Mulch heavily.

Watering
- Water deeply and frequently—consistent moisture is required for good flowering.

Fertilizing
- If leaves yellow, spray the plant with a water-soluble fertilizer for acid-loving plants or a formula for flowering plants that contains iron.

Suggestions for Vigorous Growth
- Stake individual stems if needed.
- Cut down flower spikes right after blooming; most plants will then rebloom although with shorter new spikes.

Easy Tip

Foxglove plants live only about three years, so letting them reseed is the best way to keep them in your garden.

- Leave second flush of flowers to reseed.
- If mulch is thick, pull it back to allow seeds to reach the soil.
- Lift out crowded seedlings in very early spring and replant.

Pest Control
- Foxglove has very few pests, except for slugs, which can be controlled organically (using plates of water mixed with yeast, in which they'll drown) or chemically; check with your Extension Agent.

Complementary Plants
- Plant with ferns, bleeding hearts, and cardinal flowers.
- Plant to add height to shady borders and cottage gardens.

Recommended Selections
- *Digitalis* x *mertonensis* is called the strawberry foxglove because its blooms are a delicious shade that will remind you of crushed strawberries.

Geranium

Pelargonium species and hybrids

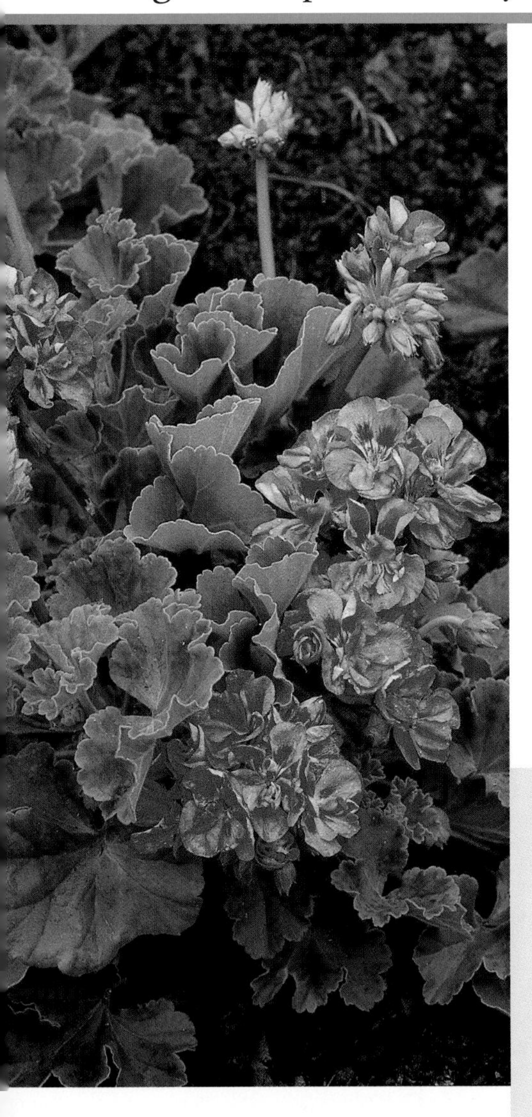

A Favorite Showy Annual Great for Containers

I can't imagine a summer without geraniums. I always grow them in containers so I can move them to the porch during long rainy spells, when they would otherwise stop blooming and sulk. But now seed-grown varieties in interesting colors are available, inexpensive, and small enough for you to plant a bed of just geraniums. These usually are sold in packs of four or six.

Top Reasons to Plant

- Bright, showy clusters of blooms
- Wide range of colors
- Long blooming season
- Good in window boxes and planters
- Attracts hummingbirds
- Roots easily for potted plants in winter

Useful Hint

In the cooler parts of the state, try delicate-looking ivy geraniums in hanging baskets.

Bloom Color
Red, orange, salmon, pink, lavender, or white; some mottled or bicolored

Bloom Period
Spring until fall

Height/Width
12 inches to 3 feet x 14 to 24 inches

Planting Location
- Rich, moist soil amended with organic matter to ensure good drainage for garden plantings
- Morning sun and afternoon shade
- Ivy geraniums need mostly shade, especially in hotter areas of the state.

Planting
- For containers, use a packaged potting mix.
- Space plants so air circulates between them—1 to 2 feet apart depending on the type.
- Work a pelleted, slow-release fertilizer into the soil.
- Water well after planting.
- Mulch lightly.

Watering
- Water regularly so soil never dries out.

Fertilizing
- Feed geraniums in pots weekly with a water-soluble fertilizer made for blooming plants.
- Place more pelleted, slow-release fertilizer around bedding geraniums in midsummer.

Easy Tip
Take cuttings in fall—they root easily—and overwinter in a sunny windowsill or greenhouse for early flowers next spring.

Suggestions for Vigorous Growth
- The key to success is pinching the tips of young plants regularly to make them branch and thus produce more flowers.
- If stems rot in garden plantings, dig up the plants and dispose of them.
- Keep old flowers cut off to encourage new blooms.

Pest Control
- If leaves turn yellow, spray with chelated iron.

Complementary Plants
- Mix with dusty miller in containers, letting *Vinca major* trail over the edges.

Recommended Selections
- 'Eyes Right' has pink blooms accented with a red eye.

Globe Amaranth

Gomphrena globosa

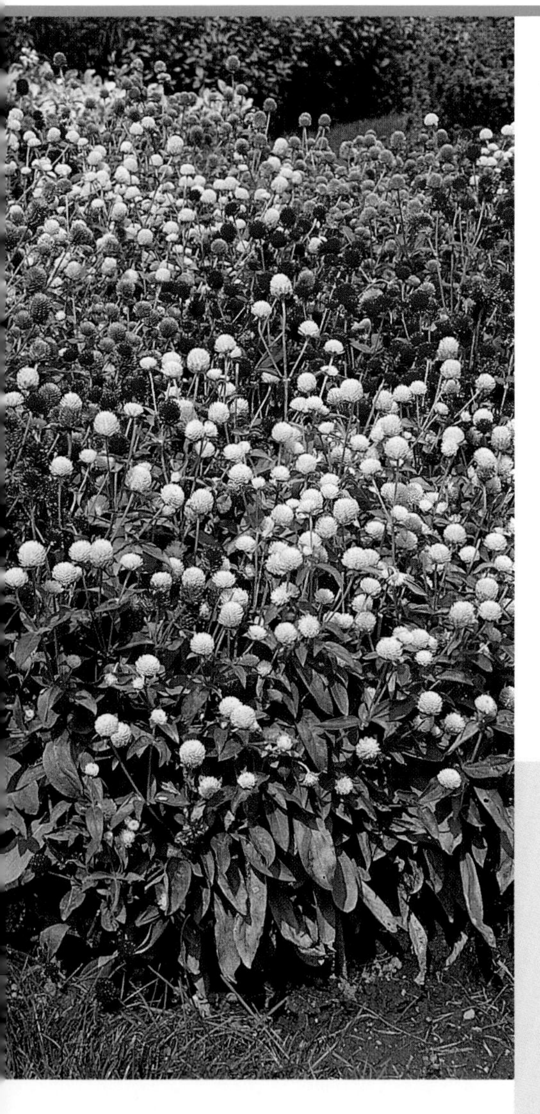

An Annual That Laughs at Tennessee Heat and Humidity

When I first fell in love with this plant—because of how it laughs at our hottest weather—I knew it would never become a hit unless it got a common name. Fortunately, gomphrena (pronounced gom-FREE-nuh) is now called globe amaranth by everyone but me—old habits die hard. It has a rounded shape and is topped all summer with little ball-like flowers that remind me of the ones on red clover.

Top Reasons to Plant

- Tolerates heat and humidity
- Bushels of blooms all summer long
- Good cut flower
- Good dried flower
- Easy to grow
- Drought tolerant when established

Useful Hint

The scarlet flowers of *Gomphrena haageana* 'Strawberry Fields' make a wonderful accent in the garden.

Bloom Color
White, purple, pink, orange-salmon, or red

Bloom Period
Summer to fall

Height/Width
10 to 24 inches x 12 to 16 inches

Planting Location
- Average to poor soil that drains rapidly
- Full sun

Planting
- Plant after the weather is consistently warm—usually May.
- Space plants 1 foot apart.
- Mix pelleted, slow-release fertilizer into the soil in the planting hole.
- Water well after planting.
- Mulch lightly.

Watering
- Once established, plants need water only during dry spells.

Fertilizing
- Fertilize seldom, and if slow-release fertilizer was used at planting, probably not at all.
- If leaves look pale, apply a water-soluble fertilizer, such as 20-20-20.

Easy Tip
The blooms dry right on the plant and can be used for winter arrangements.

Suggestions for Vigorous Growth
- Cut flowers for drying when half open and hang them upside down in a warm, dry place.

Pest Control
- Stippled leaves may mean spider mites.
- Test for spider mites by holding a piece of white paper under the suspected leaf and thumping the leaf. If the "dust" that falls begins to move, it's spider mites.
- Pick off affected leaves, and remove severely infested plants.
- Prevent spider mites by spraying water once a week under the lower leaves of the plants.

Complementary Plants
- Use with any white-flowered annuals or perennials for an especially nice effect.

Recommended Selections
- 'Lavender Lady' produces pale-violet blooms on a plant about 2 feet tall.

Goldenrod

Solidago species and hybrids

A Wonderful Garden Perennial from a Native "Weed"

You may still be thinking of goldenrod as a "weed" that grows too tall, spreads like crazy, and causes hay fever. But plant breeders have once again taken a familiar native and made it a wonderful garden plant. They've developed cultivars that are shorter and more manageable than the species, but still undemanding. Goldenrod is a reliable performer in almost any soil condition from soggy to bone-dry—and it induces no sneezing.

Useful Hint

Whatever you've heard, goldenrod has never been guilty of causing sneezing and watery eyes—they're brought on by other plants that grow nearby in the wild.

Top Reasons to Plant

- Tolerates almost any soil
- Gorgeous fall blooms
- Easy to grow
- Good cut flower
- Drought tolerant when established
- Few pests and diseases
- Mixes well with other fall-bloomers

Bloom Color
Shades of yellow

Bloom Period
Late summer to fall

Height/Width
1 to 5 feet x 1 to 3 feet

Planting Location
- Average to poor soil that is well drained
- Full sun to a little shade

Planting
- Set out plants from spring until fall.
- Space plants 12 to 18 inches apart.
- Water well.

Watering
- Once established, goldenrod tolerates drought.

Fertilizing
- For the first two years, fertilize once in early spring with a pelleted, slow-release fertilizer used at *half* the label recommendation.
- Mature plants should not need fertilizer.

Suggestions for Vigorous Growth
- Clip off spent blooms to promote repeat flowering and to prevent hybrids from reseeding—offspring are not like their parents.
- If new plants pop up, dig them up if they're in the wrong spot and replant them elsewhere.

Easy Tip

Goldenrod is perfect for naturalizing in meadows.

- If the center of the clump dies out, dig the plant up and divide it in spring, discarding the center.

Pest Control
- If powdery mildew appears, thin plants to increase air circulation.

Complementary Plants
- Goldenrod goes well with asters, boltonia, ornamental grasses, and chrysanthemums, all of which flower about the same time.
- Looks great with black-eyed Susan, purple coneflower, and coreopsis, which flower earlier but enjoy the same conditions.

Recommended Selections
- 'Golden Dwarf', 'Peter Pan', and 'Golden Baby' are delightful dwarf cultivars.
- 'Golden Wings' grows 5 feet tall and will knock your socks off.

Heucherа

Heuchera species and hybrids

A Perennial with Gorgeous Foliage and Bonus Flowers

Anyone who thinks flowers are necessary for a plant to look fabulous hasn't been introduced to heuchera. I've grown heucheras that had green leaves with red veins and silver blotches, deep purple leaves with silver markings, and silver leaves with purple veins. Of the two most common species, the one with the best blooms is *Heuchera sanguinea* and its related hybrids—often called coral bells. I like to plant both.

Top Reasons to Plant

- Beautiful foliage in varied color combinations
- Delicate sprays of colorful blooms
- Attracts hummingbirds
- Good cut flower
- Prefers shade
- Excellent near paths and patios where foliage can be seen
- Few pests or diseases
- Likes moist situations

Useful Hint

Heuchera americana, a native referred to as alumroot, has even more spectacular foliage than the more commonly grown coral bells.

Bloom Color
White, pink, or red

Bloom Period
Spring

Height/Width
1 to 2 feet x 12 to 18 inches

Planting Location
- Moist, well-drained soil, with compost or coarse sand added
- Shade or partial shade

Planting
- Set out in spring for best response, but heucheras may be planted until late summer.
- Space plants 8 to 12 inches apart.
- Water well after planting.
- Mulch well.

Watering
- Keep soil moist but never saturated.

Fertilizing
- Fertilize in early spring with half an inch of compost or a pelleted, slow-release plant food at *half* the amount recommended on the label.

Suggestions for Vigorous Growth
- Cut faded flowers with their stems to keep plants neat and to encourage reblooming.
- Renew mulch each year.

Easy Tip

Try cutting a few stems from established heucheras to use in flower arrangements.

- Divide clumps in early spring every third year, and replant immediately.
- When dividing, take care to break the plant apart rather than cut through the crown.
- If older plants develop woody stems and sprawl about, dig them up and replant a little deeper.

Pest Control
- Heucheras have few insect or disease problems.

Complementary Plants
- Plant with foamflower, creeping phlox, bleeding heart, ferns, or hostas.

Recommended Selections
- The tall flower spikes of 'Raspberry Regal' make ideal cut flowers.
- 'Pewter Veil' has stunning foliage.

Hosta

Hosta species and hybrids

A Perennial That Belongs in Every Shady Garden

If I were to recommend only one plant for a shady yard, it would be hosta. This plant has it all, starting with its great-looking leaves in shades of gold, green, cream, and yellow variegation—even blue, though many of the blue cultivars do better farther north. And don't overlook the blooms, beloved by butterflies. Hostas also vary in size from miniature to 5 feet wide. Even if you plant dozens, you'll have plenty of variety.

Top Reasons to Plant

- Beautiful foliage in many colors
- Loves shade
- Attracts butterflies
- Good foliage for flower arrangements
- Mixes well with shade annuals, such as impatiens
- Good interplanted with daffodils to hide their dying foliage

Useful Hint

Hostas are now being bred for interesting flowers, many with fragrance.

Bloom Color
White, lavender, or purple

Bloom Period
Late spring to fall

Height/Width
6 inches to 3 feet x 1 to 5 feet

Planting Location
- Rich, organic soil that drains well
- Shade or partial shade

Planting
- Space hostas 1 to 3 feet apart to accommodate their mature spread—they don't like to be moved.
- Fertilize with a pelleted, slow-release fertilizer worked into the planting hole.
- Water well after planting.
- Mulch well unless slugs are known to be a problem.

Watering
- Growth is best with consistent moisture.
- But hostas tolerate soil that dries out between waterings.
- Water when rainfall is less than an inch per week.

Fertilizing
- Apply a slow-release fertilizer around each plant when leaves appear in spring.

Suggestions for Vigorous Growth
- Cut down flower stalks as they fade so seeds don't form and sap the plant's energy.

Easy Tip

If slugs are a problem in your yard, try mulching hostas with pine straw—the slugs don't like its prickly texture.

- Avoid dividing hostas; it takes a year or two for them to recover.
- Add mulch as needed.

Pest Control
- Holes in leaves are usually caused by slugs.
- Try homemade slug traps (saucers of beer, yeast water, or an upturned grapefruit).
- Also try mulching with pine straw.
- If slugs are still a problem, consult a garden center about controls.

Complementary Plants
- Hostas are beautiful massed alone in shady beds.
- Use as accents with ferns, impatiens, and caladiums.

Recommended Selections
- 'Francee' is my all-time favorite for its deep-green leaves edged in crisp white.
- 'Patriot' is similar with a wider white margin.
- 'Grand Tiara' has a bold gold edge.
- 'Tatoo' has green and gold foliage with the outline of a maple leaf in the center.

Impatiens

Impatiens walleriana

An Annual That Provides Super Color in the Shade

Impatiens—or Busy Lizzie, as your Great Aunt Flo probably called them—need no introduction to anyone with a shady yard. This plant is the standby for shade because it's attractive, easy to grow, and covered with flowers from the time you plant it until it's struck down by frost. Impatiens are as at home in containers as they are in flower beds. And they make an impressive show in both places.

Top Reasons to Plant

- Lots of flowers in lots of colors
- Loves shade
- Easy to grow
- Few pests and diseases
- Long season of bloom
- Doesn't require deadheading—it's self-cleaning!
- Cuttings root easily to produce more plants
- Attracts hummingbirds and butterflies

Bloom Color
White, pink, rose, lavender, red, orange, salmon, and bicolors

Bloom Period
Midspring to frost

Height/Width
6 to 36 inches x 8 to 24 inches

Planting Location
- Rich, moist soil enriched with organic matter
- Shade or partial shade

Planting
- Set plants out after all chance of frost has passed.
- Place plants about 10 inches apart.
- Mix pelleted, slow-release fertilizer into the soil.
- Water well after planting.
- Mulch with 2 inches of organic mulch.

Watering
- Keep the soil constantly moist.
- Consider watering impatiens with a soaker hose if they are sited under trees.

Fertilizing
- Every two weeks during the growing season, apply a water-soluble fertilizer made for blooming plants.

Useful Hint

Hybrid impatiens are available in a variety of heights, but it's my experience that in a rainy summer, they all grow tall.

Easy Tip

Root cuttings to increase your collection of plants—they root easily in water.

Suggestions for Vigorous Growth
- Ample water and frequent fertilization are the keys to success.
- Pinch plants back anytime they look leggy.
- Reseeding can occur, but remove those plants; they won't come true to their parent.

Pest Control
- Slugs may appear in wet weather.
- Spider mites may appear in very dry weather.
- Ask your garden center or Extension Agent about chemical controls if homemade traps don't control the slugs and spraying the plants with water doesn't get rid of the spider mites.

Complementary Plants
- Use impatiens with ferns, hostas, and caladiums to brighten a bed.
- Mass white or pastel shades for viewing from the patio or window.

Recommended Selections
- 'Victorian Rose' has double flowers and looks nice in hanging baskets.

Lenten Rose

Helleborus orientalis

A Shade-Loving Perennial That Blooms in Winter

Don't let anyone convince you that because it's winter, you can't have flowers blooming. Prove them wrong with lenten rose. This evergreen perennial is a standout in deep shade—or any other type of shade. The romantic-looking single flowers come in shades of green, cream, and pink and are often spotted inside. Look for some of the new strains and hybrids hitting the market—they've been selected for intriguing colors.

Top Reasons to Plant

- Late-winter blooms
- Loves shade
- Pest and disease free
- Reseeds freely
- Good cut flower
- Easy to grow
- Flowers change color as they mature
- Handsome foliage after bloom

Useful Hint

Place lenten roses where they can be seen in winter.

Bloom Color
White, lime, rose, or maroon

Bloom Period
Late winter to spring

Height/Width
14 to 18 inches x 12 to 18 inches

Planting Location
- Well-drained, deep, fertile soil amended with organic matter
- Full to partial shade
- Choose location carefully so winter sun doesn't burn leaves and flowers.

Planting
- Set out container-grown plants in early spring.
- Transplant seedlings from around established mature plants when they're 4 inches tall.
- Space plants 18 to 24 inches apart.
- Mulch with organic matter, such as pine straw.

Watering
- Plant in moisture-retaining soil that's mulched; lenten roses prefer consistent moisture but are surprisingly tolerant of dry weather.
- Water enough to keep the soil moist when plants are young and during droughts.

Fertilizing
- Fertilize sparingly if at all—the decaying mulch usually provides sufficient nutrients.

Easy Tip

Once you plant lenten rose, you'll have it forever because it reseeds, though not aggressively—even producing new color combinations.

Suggestions for Vigorous Growth
- Evergreen leaves can sometimes suffer winter damage; clip them off as flowers appear so the flowers can shine.
- Lenten rose grows slowly and seldom needs dividing.
- Pull mulch back as seeds mature to allow the plants to reseed.

Pest Control
- Lenten rose has no serious pests.

Complementary Plants
- Plant with ajuga, primroses, violets, and ferns for a nice look.
- Try with spring-flowering shrubs such as azaleas and pieris.

Recommended Selections
- 'Royal Heritage' comes in a wide range of sumptuous colors.

Madagascar Periwinkle

Catharanthus roseus

A Heat-Loving Annual That's Perky in August

In August, when temperature and humidity both hover around 90 degrees Fahrenheit—and other annuals look as tired as you feel—Madagascar periwinkle still appears perky and fresh. It has a constantly neat appearance, with glossy green leaves and flowers that simply fall off when they fade. And it blooms all summer—in the ground or in a variety of containers. This is the one annual I'm never without.

Useful Hint

When you go to the nursery, be sure not to confuse Madagascar periwinkle with the perennial ground cover vinca, which may also be called periwinkle.

Top Reasons to Plant

- Loves heat and humidity
- Looks fresh all summer
- Easy to grow
- Good in both containers and the garden
- Ground cover types look excellent in hanging baskets
- Needs little water once established

Bloom Color
White, pink, or lavender; some with darker eyes

Bloom Period
Spring to fall

Height/Width
4 inches to 2 feet x 8 inches to $1^1/_2$ feet

Planting Location
- Well-drained soil
- Packaged potting mix when planting in containers
- Full sun or light shade part of the day

Planting
- Plant after the weather is truly warm—Madagascar periwinkle loves heat.
- Mix a timed-release fertilizer into the soil at planting.
- Space plants 8 to 18 inches apart, depending on variety.
- Water well after planting.

Watering
- In the garden, established plants manage on rainfall.
- In containers, water plants often so they don't wilt.

Fertilizing
- In August, scatter slow-release fertilizer on top of the soil.
- *Or* fertilize each month with a water-soluble fertilizer for flowering plants.

Easy Tip
Madagascar periwinkle thoughtfully drops its blooms when they fade, saving you the trouble of deadheading.

Suggestions for Vigorous Growth
- Occasionally pinch the tips of stems to encourage branching.
- If leaves yellow when temperatures remain below 70 degrees Fahrenheit, douse the plants with 1 tablespoon of chelated iron mixed with a gallon of water.
- If mature plants develop yellow leaves during warm weather, it is a sign of disease—discard the affected plants.

Pest Control
- Watch out for slugs and snails; they munch holes in the leaves.
- Pick them off by hand or use copper strips as barriers.

Complementary Plants
- Periwinkles with "eyes" look nice paired with snapdragons and wax begonias that are the same color as the eyes.

Recommended Selections
- I always plant 'Parasol', which has extra-large white flowers, each with a red eye.

Marigold

Tagetes species and hybrids

A Favorite Summer Annual That Brightens the Garden

I'd always grown dwarf marigolds because I didn't like to stake the tall ones. Then Sanford Deck, the "flower man" at the Senior Neighbors complex in Chattanooga, insisted I try 'Inca Yellow' marigolds. Variously called American or African marigolds, these won't get beaten over by thunderstorms, even if not staked, claimed Mr. Deck. I tried them—he was right—I've grown them ever since.

Top Reasons to Plant

- Bright, showy blooms
- Good cut flower
- Easy to grow from seed, either inside or out
- Comes in a wide range of heights
- Drought tolerant when established
- Few pests and diseases
- Excellent for a child's garden

Bloom Color
Yellow, burgundy, orange, or cream

Bloom Period
Summer till fall

Height/Width
6 inches to 3 feet x 10 inches to 3 feet

Planting Location
- Average soil with a thin layer of organic matter worked in
- Full sun

Planting
- Start seeds indoors one month before you plan to set them out.
- *Or* seed directly into the garden just after the last frost.
- Thin seedlings or space plants 6, 10, or 18 inches apart, depending on the type.
- Water well after planting.
- Mulch lightly.

Watering
- Let soil dry out slightly between waterings.
- Do not overwater; too much water results in leaf growth with fewer flowers and may cause diseases or root rot.
- Avoid overhead sprinklers.
- Don't water late in the day.

Useful Hint

There's always something new in the marigold line, so be sure to try a few new hybrids every year.

Easy Tip

'Inca Yellow' marigolds are tall but stand up to thunderstorms without any staking.

Fertilizing
- Fertilize once a month or less with a liquid plant food for blooming plants.

Suggestions for Vigorous Growth
- Pinch plants as they grow to promote branching and more flowers.
- Water and fertilize carefully.
- Pick off faded flowers.

Pest Control
- Slugs can devour tender, young marigolds—use barrier methods to control them rather than pelleted poisons that may harm pets and birds.

Complementary Plants
- Dwarf varieties are nice along edges of containers that also hold zinnias, Madagascar periwinkle, short ornamental grasses, and other plants that like a dry environment.
- Taller varieties look good in mixed flower and herb beds with other sun lovers.

Recommended Selections
- I wouldn't be without 'Climax' and the Inca II series because of the very large flowers they produce.

Moss Rose

Portulaca grandiflora

A Tough Little Annual That's Bright and Carefree

I defy anyone to talk about portulaca without using the words "cute" and "perky." Add to that "low maintenance." The low-growing, fleshy foliage of moss rose is also covered by some of the most brilliant flower colors around—at least on sunny days. Moss rose isn't fond of rain or overcast skies. And it stops blooming when autumn days turn chilly. If you need a carefree summer flower, moss rose delivers.

Top Reasons to Plant

- Thrives in hot, dry, sunny locations
- Bright, showy blooms in many colors
- Good in hanging baskets
- Easy to grow
- Needs no grooming
- Attracts few pests
- Drought tolerant when established

Bloom Color
White, bright shades of red, yellow, orange, pink, or purple

Bloom Period
All summer

Height/Width
3 to 6 inches x 12 to 24 inches

Planting Location
- Sandy soil, with coarse sand added to soil that's not naturally sandy
- In containers, with coarse sand added to potting mix
- Full sun

Planting
- Start seeds indoors in a warm spot about four weeks before the last frost date.
- Set plants out several weeks after the last frost, when the weather has settled and become warm.
- *Or* purchase bedding plants for the garden and for hanging baskets.
- Mix pelleted, slow-release fertilizer into the soil at planting.
- Do not mulch; the sun must warm the soil.

Watering
- Once plants are established, let the soil dry out between waterings.

Useful Hint

Put portulaca in the dry spaces between the driveway and sidewalk, using a mix of colors.

Easy Tip

This is one tough little plant, thriving in those hot, dry spots many other annuals shun.

Fertilizing
- Every two or three weeks, use a balanced, water-soluble fertilizer, such as 20-20-20, or one that's made for flowering plants.

Suggestions for Vigorous Growth
- Allow moss rose to thrive in warm soil and sun.
- Don't overwater.

Pest Control
- Aphids and thrips may occur.
- Spray aphids and thrips with insecticidal soap.
- For thrips, put up yellow sticky bags.
- If flowers abort or open with distortions, thrips are the likely culprits—replace the plants; this pest is difficult to control in annuals.

Complementary Plants
- Use in rock gardens with other low-growing creepers.

Recommended Selections
- 'Sundial Peach', an All-America Selections winner, features 2-inch, double flowers that open a long time.

New Guinea Impatiens

Impatiens hawkeri

A Glamorous Annual Impatiens That Shows Off in the Sun

Impatiens and New Guinea impatiens flowers are somewhat similar, but that is where the likeness ends. New Guineas are grown mostly for their jazzy, variegated foliage and the showy colors of their flowers. They're ideal where you want plants that create a festive feeling and call attention to themselves. Unlike *Impatiens walleriana*, New Guinea impatiens—introduced into this country in the 1970s—are not shade plants.

Top Reasons to Plant

- Tropical look
- Striking variegated foliage
- Large flowers in showy colors
- Likes mostly sun
- Few pests and diseases
- Great in containers near the pool or deck
- Attracts hummingbirds

Useful Hint

New Guinea impatiens like a bit of afternoon shade, but they do best in mostly sunny spots.

Bloom Color
White, red, pink, or salmon with leaves that are green or red-bronze, some variegated with creamy yellow

Bloom Period
Summer to first frost

Height/Width
12 to 20 inches x 12 to 15 inches

Planting Location
- Good garden soil enriched with plenty of organic matter
- Full sun or a few hours of late-afternoon shade
- Large (3-gallon) tubs or containers filled with a peat-based potting mix with rotted compost added

Planting
- Set plants out after all danger of frost has passed.
- Space plants 12 to 15 inches apart in the garden.
- Use 3 plants per 5-gallon container.
- Water well using a water-soluble root stimulator and mulch well.

Watering
- Keep well watered.

Fertilizing
- Water with water-soluble fertilizer, such as 20-20-20, every other week, alternating with 10-56-0.
- If leaves turn pale or yellow (unless they're supposed to be yellow), fertilize the plant more often.

Easy Tip
The variety 'Tango Improved' may be grown from seed started indoors a few weeks before the last frost.

Suggestions for Vigorous Growth
- Pinch plants when they are 4 inches tall.
- Pinch thereafter as needed to keep a bushy shape.
- Flowers fall off on their own, so no deadheading is needed.

Pest Control
- Few insects or diseases bother New Guineas, except for spider mites in dry conditions.
- Spray water on leaves at least weekly to prevent spider mites.

Complementary Plants
- For an instant trip to the tropics, plant New Guineas with cannas and agapanthus.
- Use New Guineas as a bridge between blooms in a sunny perennial bed.

Recommended Selections
- 'Tonga' has bronze and green leaves with lavender and purple flowers.

Ornamental Cabbage

Brassica oleracea

A Novelty Annual That Brightens the Fall

It wasn't many years ago that gardens planted in fall were filled only with vegetables. Now the beginning of football season sends us to nurseries for plants that provide color in our yards until Christmas and even spring. Ornamental cabbage and kale (which has lacy, fringed leaves) aren't as hardy as pansies, but they have novelty on their side, making them great for anyone who wants something different.

Top Reasons to Plant

- Provides color from fall until winter
- Mixes well with other fall bloomers
- Novelty plant for those wanting something different
- Leaves good for indoor arrangements

Useful Hint

As days and nights grow cooler, the coloration of purple-leafed ornamental cabbages deepens until it's almost luminous.

Bloom Color
Grown for fringed wavy leaves of green, white, red, and purple

Bloom Period
Fall until mid- or late winter, or spring until early summer

Height/Width
6 to 12 inches x 8 to 12 inches

Planting Location
- Average, well-drained garden soil
- Sun or a few hours of late-afternoon shade

Planting
- To grow from seed, sow them in the garden in summer and keep the seedbed moist by laying a board over the seeds until they sprout.
- Buy plants from a nursery as early as possible.
- Thin seedlings or space purchased plants 1 foot apart.
- Be sure transplants sit directly at ground level.
- Mix a pelleted, slow-release fertilizer into the soil at planting time.
- Mulch to moderate soil temperatures and to retain moisture.

Watering
- Water plants frequently until they become established or the ground freezes.
- Water weekly during fall.

Fertilizing
- Water with water-soluble plant food, such as 20-20-20, every three weeks until the ground freezes.

Easy Tip
Plant ornamental cabbage as soon as it's available at nurseries—the earlier it's planted, the more cold it will withstand.

Suggestions for Vigorous Growth
- Feed and water correctly.

Pest Control
- Ornamental cabbage and kale may attract cabbageworms, slugs, snails, and cutworms. For these pests, use barrier methods and plant collars to prevent damage.
- Exclude egg-laying butterflies by covering plants with insect-barrier fabric or spray with *Bacillus thuringiensis* (Bt) to control cabbageworm larvae when they hatch.
- Grow ornamental cabbage and kale away from edible varieties.

Complementary Plants
- Ornamental cabbage and kale are good companions to complementary-colored chrysanthemums.
- They look attractive planted in front of ornamental grasses.

Recommended Selections
- 'Nagoya' kale has especially frilly leaves.
- Color Up series hybrid cabbage—in pink, white, or red—has intense coloration.

Ornamental Pepper

Capsicum annuum

A Cheerful Annual That Sports Multicolored Fruit

One summer we were living in a rented house in Johnson City. There was no room for a vegetable garden, although there was a sunny flower bed near the front door. So I decided to grow cherry tomatoes and ornamental peppers among the annual flowers. I wasn't sure what the neighborhood reaction would be. It turned out that everyone loved the little peppers that turned from cream to purple.

Top Reasons to Plant

- Showy, unusual little fruit
- Good in containers
- Mixes well with annual flowers
- Color peaks in fall
- Attracts butterflies
- Provides an exotic touch to the garden

Useful Hint

For an unusual look, mix ornamental peppers into plantings with flowers in compatible colors.

Bloom Color
White or purple flowers followed by peppers that ripen to red, purple, yellow, or orange

Bloom Period
Summer to frost

Height/Width
4 inches to 3 feet x 6 inches to 2 feet

Planting Location
- Moderately rich soil that stays evenly moist and is amended with organic matter
- Full sun

Planting
- Start seeds indoors in a very warm, sunny environment six weeks before the last expected frost.
- Do not plant outside until the soil temperature is at least 60 degrees Fahrenheit—wait till settled, warm weather has arrived.
- Space plants 10 to 16 inches apart.
- Water well after planting.
- Mulch well.

Watering
- Keep well watered; plants stunted by lack of water will not fruit.
- Thin leaves and heavy fruiting increase peppers' need for water.
- Container-grown peppers may need water daily in hot weather to prevent wilting.

Fertilizing
- Use a water-soluble fertilizer, such as 20-20-20, once weekly.

Easy Tip
Ornamental peppers make great container plants—and the peppers are edible!

Suggestions for Vigorous Growth
- Keep plants received as winter gifts in a warm, sunny room until frost-free weather arrives.
- Repot container plants in a peat-based potting mix, and set outside during the summer.
- Use plastic pots; their dark surfaces keep roots warmer and more evenly moist than clay pots.

Pest Control
- Whiteflies can be a serious pest; at the first sign of infestation, hand pick affected leaves, and put up yellow sticky traps.

Complementary Plants
- Grow with Wave™ series petunias and Madagascar periwinkle for summer-long color.

Recommended Selections
- 'Variegata' has white, lavender, purple, and green foliage, with purple peppers that ripen to red.

Pansy

Viola × wittrockiana

A Cheerful Little Annual to Brighten the Winter

I've been gardening long enough to remember winters without pansies. Then two things happened. Gardeners became more interested in having something blooming in their yards year-round. And people noticed that theme parks—such as Six Flags and Disney World—were filled with colorful flowers every month of the year. In response, plant breeders developed pansies that are quite cold hardy.

Top Reasons to Plant

- Flowers during winter
- Perky little blooms
- Wide range of colors
- Excellent interplanted with spring bulbs
- Good in containers
- Nice cut flowers in small vases
- Will lure you out of doors in winter

Useful Hint

Pansies won't bloom during winter's coldest weather, but the flowers return quickly during warm spells.

Bloom Color
Red, yellow, orange, blue, violet, or white, both single colors and bicolors, many with "faces"

Bloom Period
Fall through early summer

Height/Width
8 inches x 8 inches

Planting Location
- Well-drained soil rich in organic matter
- Sun in winter and partial shade in spring

Planting
- Set out plants in early fall—the sooner they're planted, the more their roots grow, and the hardier they will be.
- Space the plants no more than 5 inches apart—they won't grow and fill in over winter, which is when you want the show.
- Water well with a root stimulator.
- Mulch.

Watering
- Pansies require consistent moisture, so they may need watering several times a week in windy weather.

Fertilizing
- Use a water-soluble fertilizer for blooming plants every other week until the ground freezes.
- During winter thaws, fertilize again.

Suggestions for Vigorous Growth
- Keep old flowers trimmed off to extend the bloom season.

Easy Tip
Mulch after plants are established to protect roots and prevent them from being heaved out of the ground by frost.

Pest Control
- Slugs can be a major pest—set up barriers, such as copper strips, to control them.
- Overwatering, planting too closely, and damp weather conditions can contribute to an assortment of fungal diseases; be sure your pansies have good air circulation and well-drained soil.

Complementary Plants
- Combine pansies with snapdragons and foxglove for a bright spring show.
- Plant pansies in coordinating colors among your daffodils and tulips.

Recommended Selections
- 'Jolly Joker' is an eye-boggling orange and purple.
- The Majestic Giant series has 4-inch flowers.

Pentas

Pentas lanceolata

A Lush Annual That Gives the Garden a Tropical Flair

In our current rush to grow lush-looking tropical plants, pentas is finally starting to get the attention it deserves. That's because it's easy to grow, doesn't mind the steamiest summer, and blooms for a long time. Besides, it's pretty. The round flower clusters—consisting of dozens of tiny, star-shaped blossoms (giving rise to the common names star flower and Egyptian star cluster)—are often red or pink, adding to the "hot" look.

Top Reasons to Plant

- Tropical-looking clusters of blossoms
- Attracts butterflies and hummingbirds
- Thrives on heat and humidity
- Easy to grow
- Long bloom period
- Good in containers
- Few pests and diseases
- Fragrant flowers

Useful Hint

Pentas draws butterflies to your yard like a magnet.

Bloom Color
Pink, rose, purple, or white

Bloom Period
Summer

Height/Width
14 to 24 inches x 10 to 14 inches

Planting Location
- Well-drained, very rich soil containing plenty of compost and ground bark or rotted sawdust if drainage is a problem
- Sun

Planting
- Pentas are widely available at nurseries, but if you want to grow them from seed, sow them indoors in a cool (60 degrees F.) environment ten weeks before the last frost.
- Set plants out about three weeks after the last frost, when the soil has warmed.
- Work a pelleted, slow-release fertilizer into the soil.
- Space plants 6 to 8 inches apart.
- Water well after planting.
- Mulch generously.

Watering
- Water pentas several times a week in dry weather.
- Water container-grown pentas often to ensure that the plant doesn't wilt.

Fertilizing
- Fertilize between blooming periods with a water-soluble plant food made for flowering plants.

Easy Tip
Mulch heavily to reduce the need for watering.

Suggestions for Vigorous Growth
- Keep spent flowers picked off.
- Pinch young plants once to encourage bushy plants with multiple flower heads.
- As plants grow, pinch to maintain shape.
- Cuttings root easily in potting soil all summer.
- If pentas gets starved and thirsty, it will grow woody—cut the plant back, and it may rejuvenate itself.

Pest Control
- Slugs may eat pentas but they will eat other plants first.

Complementary Plants
- Combine with petunias, asparagus fern, and red fountain grass in a huge urn for a special patio centerpiece.

Recommended Selections
- 'Pink Profusion' has a pretty color.
- 'Ruby Glow' is good with yellow coreopsis.

Peony

Paeonia lactiflora

An Old-Fashioned, Long-Lived Perennial That Belongs in Every Garden

There's no plant that evokes more memories than peonies. Your grandmother probably grew them; so did your mother. And while this generation turns to "new and improved" peonies, we couldn't do without the old-fashioned ones. Peonies take a while to establish, but once they do, they practically live forever, providing armloads of lush blossoms year after year.

Top Reasons to Plant

- Beautiful spring blooms
- Fragrant flowers (many varieties)
- Handsome shrublike look after bloom
- Excellent cut flower
- Lives many years
- Generally pest free

Useful Hint

Avoid letting your peony flowers end up in the mud after hard rains—choose single- instead of double-flowered types or support the plants with wire cages or hoops.

Bloom Color
Pink, purple, red, yellow, or white

Bloom Period
Late spring

Height/Width
12 to 30 inches x 12 to 30 inches

Planting Location
- Well-prepared soil, dug to 12 inches deep and amended with organic matter; peonies stay in one place for a long time, so soil preparation matters more than with most plants
- Sun or a few hours of afternoon shade

Planting
- Plant dormant roots in fall, measuring to ensure they're 1 to 2 inches below soil level.
- Plant container-grown specimens in spring, setting plants at the same level or slightly higher than they were in the pot.
- Planting too deep keeps the plant from blooming.
- Space 20 to 24 inches apart, depending on mature size.
- Water well after planting.
- Mulch well.

Watering
- Consistent moisture is critical, so use a soaker hose for best results.

Fertilizing
- Place 1/2 inch of compost on top of the soil in spring and summer.
- Apply a pelleted, slow-release fertilizer in midspring.

Easy Tip
Once established, peonies are carefree and keep getting larger and producing more flowers every year.

Suggestions for Vigorous Growth
- Use peony supports (cages or hoops) as soon as the plants begin growing.
- Peonies seldom need dividing and recover from it poorly.
- Keep in mind that peonies may take two years or more to bloom well.
- Remove spent flowers to prevent the plant from expending energy setting seeds.

Pest Control
- If leaf diseases appear or insects strike, consult the Extension Service.
- Ants crawling on the plants are not a pest—they help the flowers.

Complementary Plants
- Plant peonies alone for the best effect.
- Place them on the sunny edge of a ground cover bed.

Recommended Selections
- Early and midseason cultivars, as well as those with single flowers, are best in the warmer parts of the state.
- You still can't beat 'Festiva Maxima', an old cultivar with very fragrant, double white blooms flecked with red.

Petunia

Petunia × hybrida

An Updated Annual Offering Lots of Variety

Petunias may seem as familiar as your best friend. But today's choices aren't necessarily your mother's petunias. New hybrids are being released each year, with many of the newest types grown exclusively from cuttings, not seeds. Choose classic grandifloras for big, early flowers in baskets and boxes; add multifloras and floribundas for massing in flower beds. Fill a sunny, dry spot with the trailing Surfinia® series.

Top Reasons to Plant

- Beautiful, classic summer flower
- Wide range of colors
- Long bloom season
- Excellent in containers
- Surfinia® and Wave™ series look great in hanging baskets
- Attracts hummingbirds and butterflies
- Fragrant flowers

Bloom Color
White or every shade of rose, red, pink, purple, yellow, or bicolors

Bloom Period
Spring until frost

Height/Width
6 to 18 inches x 12 to 24 inches

Planting Location
- Average garden soil.
- Sun to partial shade; petunias can grow in full sun if they have lots of water, but they appreciate an hour or two of afternoon shade and also grow with a half day's sun.

Planting
- Set out plants after all danger of frost has passed and on into midsummer.
- Space plants 8 inches apart, slightly closer in containers.
- Mix a pelleted, slow-release fertilizer into the soil.
- Water with a transplant solution.
- Mulch lightly to moderate soil conditions.

Watering
- Water often to keep the bed or container from drying out.

Easy Tip

If the soil dries out easily and plants wilt, water, then add more mulch.

Fertilizing
- Use a water-soluble fertilizer for flowering plants every other week.

Suggestions for Vigorous Growth
- Pinch stems after the first flowers appear to encourage bushy plants and more blooms.
- Shear back leggy plants and fertilize to rejuvenate.
- Pinch off all flowers as they fade.

Pest Control
- Whiteflies may be a problem in overly dry conditions.
- Botrytis and pythium rots may occur in overly damp conditions.
- Consult the Extension Service about remedies.

Complementary Plants
- Petunias combine well with most summer annuals in coordinating colors.

Recommended Selections
- The Madonna series stands up well to heat and humidity.
- 'Super Cascade' is good for really full hanging baskets.

Useful Hint

While large grandiflora petunias are glitzy, the single multifloras aren't beaten down by rain, which is a valuable quality.

Phlox

Phlox species and hybrids

A Perennial with Outstanding Midsummer Color

Phlox are such good garden plants that there is a confusing array of them. Two species provide outstanding selections that every gardener should try. Garden phlox or summer phlox (*Phlox paniculata*) produces large, long-lasting flower clusters on 3- to 5-foot stalks. A nice variety of colors is available, and many cultivars have contrasting eyes. *Phlox maculata*, sometimes referred to as Carolina phlox, has mildew-resistant foliage.

Top Reasons to Plant

- Long season of bloom
- Large flower clusters
- Attracts hummingbirds and butterflies
- Good cut flower
- Fragrant flowers

Useful Hint

Both summer phlox and Carolina phlox stay in flower for a long time, impressing all who see them.

Bloom Color
Pink, red, white, lavender, or purple

Bloom Period
Summer

Height/Width
2 to 5 feet x 1 to 3 feet

Planting Location
- Average soil that stays moist or can be kept watered
- Full sun is fine for many cultivars, but all, especially those with deep-colored flowers, appreciate some afternoon shade.

Planting
- Set out plants in mid- to late spring.
- Space plants 18 inches apart.
- Water well.
- Mulch deeply.

Watering
- Water well in weeks with less than 1 inch of rain.

Fertilizing
- Fertilizer is not usually needed, but if plants aren't growing or blooming well, use a water-soluble fertilizer for flowering plants.

Suggestions for Vigorous Growth
- Deadhead flowers for a longer bloom period.
- Do not permit plants to self-seed; those seedlings will have magenta flowers and be so vigorous they'll crowd out the rest of the plants.
- Divide plants every three years.

Easy Tip
To avoid mildew problems, choose cultivars bred to resist the disease.

Pest Control
- Mildew is phlox's Achilles heel—buy mildew-resistant cultivars, space the plants well apart so air can circulate among them, and don't splash water on the leaves.
- If mildew develops, consult the Extension Service about controls.
- Spider mites may appear in dry weather.

Complementary Plants
- Plant at the back of a flower bed with other summer-flowering perennials.

Recommended Selections
- I can't imagine being without *Phlox maculata* 'Miss Lingard'. It has white blooms and has never mildewed in my yard.

Purple Coneflower

Echinacea purpurea

A Wonderful Perennial That Isn't Purple at All

Since the blooms of this delightful plant obviously aren't purple, my sons would always ask, "Why isn't it called pink coneflower?" But this name business gets even more confusing. There are also white cultivars. And yes, they're called white purple coneflowers. The best thing is not to worry about it. Just buy as many cultivars of this fabulous plant as you can find and for which you have sunny space.

Useful Hint

This plant has so many virtues I can't name them all—and no faults I can think of.

Top Reasons to Plant

- Long bloom season
- Likes poor soil
- Drought tolerant
- Beautiful daisylike flowers
- Attracts butterflies
- Good cut flower
- Easy to grow
- Few pests and diseases
- Excellent in naturalized settings

Bloom Color
Dusty pink or white

Bloom Period
Summer to fall

Height/Width
2 to 4 feet x 1 to 2 feet

Planting Location
- Well-drained soil not rich in organic matter
- Sun

Planting
- Plant spring through summer.
- Space clumps 18 to 24 inches apart.
- Do not bury the crown (the point where roots and stems meet) when planting.
- Mulch up to 1 inch from the stem.

Watering
- Water deeply but infrequently to encourage deep roots and drought resistance.

Fertilizing
- No fertilizer is needed except for a light dressing of compost in spring.
- Too much fertilizer results in tall stems and fewer flowers.

Suggestions for Vigorous Growth
- Keep early faded flowers picked off to encourage bloom.
- Leave the last blooms intact so that plants reseed—seedheads also attract birds.

Easy Tip
Leave the last round of flowers on the plants to produce seeds for the birds and to provide more plants.

Pest Control
- Japanese beetles may be a problem; pick off small infestations, and drown the beetles in a jar of water or oil.
- Caterpillars may be a problem since butterflies and their larvae love purple coneflower—pick them off by hand.
- Use insecticidal soap only if caterpillars are stripping the plant.

Complementary Plants
- Purple coneflower looks good in meadows or other naturalized landscapes.
- Plant in butterfly gardens with ornamental grasses, gaillardia, black-eyed Susan, and yarrow.

Recommended Selections
- My favorite pink is 'Bright Star', which blooms abundantly.

Salvia (Annual)

Salvia species and hybrids

Annual Showstoppers Offering Rich Reds and More

Although red salvia—sometimes called scarlet sage—is the best known of the annual salvias, red isn't the only color, and the familiar spiked blooms of *Salvia splendens* aren't the only form. Annual salvias are available in pink, purple, and creamy white. Texas sage (*Salvia coccinea*) sports delicate red, white, or salmon flowers. Mealycup sage (*Salvia farinacea*) comes in white and shades of blue.

Top Reasons to Plant

- Showy flowers in a wide range of colors
- Likes heat and humidity
- Easy to grow
- Attracts butterflies and hummingbirds
- Good cut flower
- Long bloom season
- Few pests and diseases

Useful Hint

The annual salvias are an appealing family of plants—they are simple to grow, like heat and sun, bloom from early summer until frost, and attract hummingbirds.

Bloom Color
Bright-red, pink, purple, or creamy white

Bloom Period
Late spring through frost

Height/Width
10 to 26 inches x 12 to 18 inches

Planting Location
- Average, well-drained soil
- Sun all or most of the day

Planting
- Start seeds indoors in a sunny, fairly warm environment ten weeks before the last frost date.
- Set out purchased plants or seedlings after all chance of frost has passed and the soil has warmed.
- Space plants 6 to 18 inches apart, depending on type.
- Add a pelleted, slow-release fertilizer to the soil at planting time and water well.

Watering
- Scarlet sage demands consistent moisture, the Texas sages less so, and mealycups prefer to dry out between waterings.

Fertilizing
- Feed every two weeks with a water-soluble fertilizer for flowering plants.

Suggestions for Vigorous Growth
- Keep fading flowers picked off, especially with scarlet sage, since once flowers mature, plants fail quickly.
- Pinch back mealycups after blooming to maintain bushiness and to keep the flowers coming.

Easy Tip
Try 'Lady in Red'—it's prettier than the usual red salvia.

Pest Control
- Few pests trouble salvia, but leaf spot and rust fungus can develop in cool weather.
- Pick off affected leaves.
- Leafhoppers and aphids can be a problem in very dry weather.
- Spray with insecticidal soap, or for severe infestations, consult the Extension Service about controls.

Complementary Plants
- Use scarlet sage with silver dusty miller and white Madagascar periwinkle.
- Plant Texas sage in front of roses.
- Mealycups look pretty among perennials and bulbs.

Recommended Selections
- *Salvia coccinea* 'Lady in Red' is, hands down, my favorite annual.

Salvia (Perennial)

Salvia species and hybrids

Showy Long-Blooming Perennials That Are True Blue

Perennial salvia is often referred to as "blue salvia," but, in addition to true blue, blooms may be purple or, less often, red, pink, or white. All have tubular flowers borne on spikes. And these excellent butterfly-attracting plants don't need much attention. There are many species of salvia—some are biennial, some are annuals, and some are tender perennials grown as annuals. Know what you're buying if you want it to be perennial.

Top Reasons to Plant

- Spikes of flowers in true-blue and related colors
- Attracts butterflies
- Good cut flower
- Long blooming season
- Easy to grow
- Few pests and diseases
- Comes in sizes and colors to fit every garden

Useful Hint

If you love blue, look in catalogs for some of the tender salvias—*Salvia patens*, *Salvia guaranitica* 'Costa Rican Form', or *Salvia sinaloensis*.

Bloom Color
Blue, purple, red, pink, or white

Bloom Period
Late spring to fall

Height/Width
1 to 2 feet x 1 to 3 feet

Planting Location
- Average, well-drained soil; work organic matter into heavy soils to improve drainage; wet soil in winter causes plants to rot.
- Sun

Planting
- Set plants out anytime after the last frost through late summer.
- Space plants 10 inches to 2 feet apart, depending on type.
- Mix a pelleted, slow-release fertilizer into the soil.
- Water and mulch well.

Watering
- Once established, salvia tolerates drought relatively well if necessary.
- Water in weeks that receive less than an inch of rain—salvia blooms better with regular moisture.

Fertilizing
- Garden plants probably won't need fertilizer.
- Feed container plants monthly with a water-soluble plant food for flowers.

Easy Tip
Instead of deadheading all summer, wait and use loppers or a string trimmer to cut off all flower stalks after flowering; the plants may then rebloom several times.

Suggestions for Vigorous Growth
- Pinch salvias each spring when they're 4 inches tall and again at 8 inches to increase bushiness and to encourage more flowers.
- Keep faded flowers cut off to encourage reblooming and to prevent seeds.
- Salvia crowns (where roots and stems meet) may become woody and need dividing every four years or so.

Pest Control
- Few pests bother this plant.

Complementary Plants
- Use in beds or borders with Russian sage, dusty miller, *Artemisia* 'Powis Castle', and pink daylilies.

Recommended Selections
- 'Blue Hill' is truly blue, a rare color in the plant kingdom.
- 'East Friesland' ('Ostfriesland') has purple flowers on an 18-inch plant.
- 'Rose Queen' is probably the best pink.

Scaevola

Scaevola hybrids

A Lovely Blue Annual Perfect for Containers and Ground Cover

Blue flowers are so hard to find—and so coveted by gardeners—that when scaevola burst onto the scene, it became an instant hit. Not all varieties have true-blue blooms—some are lavender or violet-blue—but you'll find shades ranging from pale to intense blue. This trailing plant is ideal for hanging baskets, and it forms a low mat to create an unusual annual ground cover.

Top Reasons to Plant

- Long blooming season
- Tolerates heat and humidity
- Excellent in hanging baskets, trailing 3 feet or more
- Few pests and diseases
- Excellent blue and related colors
- Attracts butterflies
- Combines well in containers with red or yellow annuals

Bloom Color
Blue to violet

Bloom Period
Late spring until frost

Height/Width
4 to 12 inches x 12 inches to 3 feet

Planting Location
- Well-drained soil enriched with organic matter
- Sun

Planting
- Set out in spring after the soil has warmed up.
- Place two or three plants in a hanging basket.
- Mix pelleted, slow-release fertilizer into the soil at planting time.
- Water well.
- Use pine straw to mulch beds.

Watering
- Keep the soil moist—the plant stops growing and blooming unless well watered.

Fertilizing
- Feed garden plants twice a month and container plants each week with a water-soluble plant food made for flowers.

Useful Hint

When you go to the garden center for plants, ask for skuh-VOH-luh, sometimes called fan flower for the shape of its blooms.

Easy Tip

Place pots of scaevola on top of a wall and let them cascade over.

Suggestions for Vigorous Growth
- Pinch tips lightly to promote bushiness when plants have 3 inches of new growth.
- Continue pinching occasionally through midsummer.
- To bring indoors for the winter, cut plant back to encourage new growth and pot up the cuttings.
- The following May, root the cuttings when outdoor temperatures reach 70-75 degrees Fahrenheit.

Pest Control
- Few pests bother scaevola.

Complementary Plants
- Pair scaevola with your favorite red or yellow annuals, such as petunia, salvia, celosia, or sunflower.

Recommended Selections
- 'Blue Wonder' and 'Blue Fans' have sky-blue flowers with white eyes.
- 'Blue Shamrock' is the most intense blue I've seen.

Sedum 'Autumn Joy'

Hylotelephium 'Autumn Joy' ('Herbstfreude')

A Valuable Perennial Interesting in All Growing Seasons

The common name, stonecrop, tells you this is a plant for a rock garden. But because it's interesting the entire growing season, 'Autumn Joy' is valuable in many garden situations. The fleshy foliage is quite a contrast to most other perennials. 'Autumn Joy' (as well as related hybrids) offers large, dense flower heads that change color as they mature. Plants grown from cuttings bloom in early fall.

Top Reasons to Plant

- Interesting foliage all summer
- Blooms that change color as they age
- Attracts butterflies
- Doesn't need fertilizer
- Cuttings root easily
- Good cut flower
- Fall blooms when few perennials have blossoms

Bloom Color
Pink or reddish shades, maturing to darker colors

Bloom Period
Late summer to fall

Height/Width
18 inches to 2 feet x 18 inches to 2 feet

Planting Location
- Well-drained garden soil, with organic matter added to improve drainage
- Sun or very light shade

Planting
- Set plants out from late spring until early fall.
- Space plants 18 inches to 2 feet apart.
- Fertilize with a water-soluble product for flowering plants.
- Mulch lightly, or not at all.

Watering
- Water regularly but moderately in weeks with less than an inch of rain.
- Allow the soil to dry between waterings.
- Shallow root systems cannot take large amounts of water when plants are small.

Fertilizing
- Do not fertilize.

Useful Hint

If your 'Autumn Joy' blooms before late summer, it was seed-grown—look for a plant grown from cuttings for fall blossoms.

Easy Tip

Root cuttings to produce more 'Autumn Joy'.

Suggestions for Vigorous Growth
- Pinch 'Autumn Joy' once in late spring and again in early summer to encourage bushiness and to keep it compact.
- If plants located in partial sun flop over, cut them back by half toward the end of June.
- Space correctly when planting, and these plants won't need dividing for many years.
- When division is required, do it in spring.

Pest Control
- Few pests or diseases bother 'Autumn Joy'.

Complementary Plants
- Mass in a bed to themselves where they can spread freely.
- Plant in perennial beds with dusty miller and *Artemisia* 'Powis Castle'.

Recommended Selections
- 'Atropurpureum' has bronze leaves and reddish flowers.
- *Hylotelephium spectabile*, a close relative, has a white cultivar, 'Iceberg', and 'Indian Chief' has blooms that start out red and fade to pink.

Shasta Daisy

Leucanthemum × superbum

A Perennial Loaded with Classic Daisies

"Daisy, Daisy, give me your answer true. I'm half crazy all for the love of you." When I was a kid and went on rides in the country with my parents, my dad always sang those words when he spied a field of wild daisies. While Shasta daisies are hybrids, they're just as carefree as roadside plants. The main difference is their larger flowers. No wonder they're as popular with seasoned gardeners as with beginners.

Top Reasons to Plant

- Romantic daisy flowers
- Loads of excellent cut flowers
- Few pests and diseases
- Reseeds readily and usually true to parent
- Long blooming season
- Gives a cottage-garden look
- Attracts butterflies

Useful Hint

Shastas are equally attractive in the garden and in arrangements.

Bloom Color
White or yellow

Bloom Period
Spring to summer

Height/Width
1 to 3 feet x 18 to 24 inches

Planting Location
- Rich, moist soil preferred, but tolerates just about any well-drained soil
- Full sun or mostly sun

Planting
- Set out container-grown Shasta daisies in spring or early summer.
- Space 18 to 24 inches apart.
- Water well with a transplant solution.
- Mulch but do not cover the crown (the point where roots and stems meet).

Watering
- Keep soil moist but not saturated for the best flowering.
- Water deeply.

Fertilizing
- No fertilizer is needed in average soil.
- Too much fertilizer causes floppy stems.

Easy Tip
Divide and replant every three years to keep Shasta daisies from dying out.

Suggestions for Vigorous Growth
- Keep flowers deadheaded or cut for arrangements.
- As flowers fade, cut down to the next viable bud to encourage reblooming.
- Clumps die out unless divided—every third year, divide and replant right away.
- Let volunteers (reseeded plants) grow unless they aren't true to the parent plants or crowd the bed.
- Stake tall varieties with flower rings, if necessary.

Pest Control
- Few insects or diseases trouble Shasta daisies.

Complementary Plants
- Plant with bearded irises and antique roses for a cottage-garden effect.

Recommended Selections
- 'Becky' is the best Shasta daisy I've ever grown. It's more vigorous, blooms later than other cultivars, and produces large flowers for a long time.

Snapdragon

Antirrhinum majus

A Colorful Annual with Blooms Beloved by Children Everywhere

I'm going to let you in on a secret. Snapdragons are listed as annuals because that's what the experts call them. But in Tennessee, they're perennials. They come back year after year unless we have an exceptionally cold winter. That means you can have perennial plants at annual prices, since they're sold in six-packs.

Useful Hint

If you have children in your life you'd like to interest in gardening, show them how to open the "jaws" of the flowers and let them snap shut again.

Top Reasons to Plant

- Bountiful stalks of flowers with a unique shape
- Good cut flower
- Perennial at annual prices
- Wide range of colors—everything except blue
- Long blooming season
- Good selection of heights for all purposes
- Attracts butterflies and hummingbirds

Bloom Color
Pink, red, purple, orange, yellow, or white in solids and bicolors

Bloom Period
Spring until frost

Height/Width
6 inches to 3 feet x 1 foot

Planting Location
- Well-drained, rich soil improved with lots of organic matter
- Sun to light shade

Planting
- Set out plants as soon as they're available—they'll tolerate spring frosts.
- Space plants 6 to 12 inches apart.
- Plant in containers using a peat-based or soil-less potting mix.
- Mix pelleted, slow-release fertilizer into the soil.
- Water well with a root stimulator.

Watering
- Water frequently until plants establish.
- Water established plants enough that they don't dry out.

Fertilizing
- Use water-soluble fertilizer for blooming plants every two weeks until flowering stops in summer.

Suggestions for Vigorous Growth
- When plants stop blooming in the summer heat, cut them back by one-third and keep them watered.
- Once plants begin growing again, resume fertilizing for fall flowers.
- Deadhead regularly to keep plants blooming.
- Cut for arrangements when one-third of the flowers on a stem are open.

Easy Tip
For a cottage garden look, mix various shades of snapdragons.

Pest Control
- Rust can be a problem.
- Look for rust-resistant varieties, use soaker hoses to water, and leave space between plants for air circulation.

Complementary Plants
- Mix yellow snapdragons with variegated *Liriope* or purple-flowered *Verbena bonariensis*.

Recommended Selections
- 'Frosty Lavender Bells' grows 8 to 10 inches tall in sun or shade and has almost cup-shaped flowers.
- 'Chinese Lanterns' has a cascading habit.

Sunflower

Helianthus annuus

A Classic Summer Annual with Lots of Brand-New Looks

Remember when sunflowers were tall and yellow and mostly grown on the edges of vegetable gardens? Have they ever changed! Now there's a color and size for every yard—creamy-white, smoky-red, orange, bronze, and red. And flowers vary from 4 inches to more than a foot across atop plants as small as 24 inches tall. Fortunately, growing these exciting new sunflowers is still as simple as child's play.

Top Reasons to Plant

- Bright summery blooms
- Wide range of colors
- Heights from 2 feet to mammoth
- Beloved by children and birds
- Good cut flower
- Easy to grow
- Drought tolerant when established
- Few pests and diseases

Useful Hint

Plant several types and colors of shorter varieties for an instant cutting garden.

Bloom Color
Yellow and brown, clear-yellow, cream, red, bronze, or orange

Bloom Period
Summer to fall

Height/Width
24 inches to 12 feet x 12 to 24 inches

Planting Location
- Best in soil enriched with organic matter
- Full sun

Planting
- Sunflowers don't always transplant well, so plant seeds outdoors where you want them to grow.
- Sow seeds after danger of frost has passed.
- Mix a handful of 6-12-12 fertilizer into prepared soil.
- Keep the soil moist until seeds sprout.
- Thin plants to 1 to 4 feet apart, depending on their mature size.

Watering
- These drought-tolerant plants require little water once established.
- But water regularly when rainfall is light for more consistent growth and bloom.

Fertilizing
- In midsummer, spread another handful of 6-12-12 in a circle 6 to 12 inches away from the stem.
- Water dry fertilizer in well.
- *Or* use a balanced, water-soluble fertilizer, such as 20-20-20, several times over the summer.

Easy Tip
If you plant sunflowers in too much shade, they'll lean toward the light and require staking.

Suggestions for Vigorous Growth
- Many of the new types have multiple flower heads and bloom longer if they're deadheaded.
- Let late flowers set seed for the birds.

Pest Control
- Sunflowers have few pest and disease problems.

Complementary Plants
- Plant shorter types with butterfly weed, coreopsis, and gaillardia.
- Plant tall types against a dark background, such as a fence or a row of evergreens, for the best effect.

Recommended Selections
- 'Moulin Rouge' has deep-red flowers and burgundy stems.
- 'Teddy Bear' has fluffy yellow flowers on 3-foot stems.
- 'Italian White' is beloved by goldfinches.

Sweet Alyssum

Lobularia maritima

A Pretty Low-Growing Annual with a Fabulous Scent

Seeing—and smelling—sweet alyssum transports you back to a quieter, slower time. This sweet little plant, covered with tiny blooms and giving off a delightful fragrance, has a wonderfully old-fashioned feel. It reminds you of your grandmother's garden, but will be right at home in yours—if you have a sunny spot in reach of the hose. Low-growing and drought tolerant, sweet alyssum brings the best of the past to the present.

Top Reasons to Plant

- Lots of tiny, showy flowers
- Wonderful fragrance
- Low growing
- Drought tolerant when established
- Attracts butterflies
- Easy to grow
- Few pests and diseases

Useful Hint

The white-flowered varieties of sweet alyssum mix well with everything and provide a fresh, clean look.

Bloom Color
White, purple, pink, or light salmon

Bloom Period
Spring to frost

Height/Width
3 to 6 inches x 12 to 18 inches

Planting Location
- Good garden soil amended with compost if the natural soil has clay or is rocky
- Sun or a little shade

Planting
- Sow seeds directly into the garden three weeks before the last expected frost.
- Purchase plants at any garden center.
- Work a pelleted, slow-release fertilizer into the soil before planting.
- Thin seedlings to 4 inches apart when they're an inch tall.
- Set purchased plants 6 to 8 inches apart.
- Water well.

Watering
- Water before the soil dries out completely.

Fertilizing
- Every two or three weeks, feed with a water-soluble fertilizer such as 20-20-20.

Suggestions for Vigorous Growth
- Once plants are established, mulch to help moderate soil conditions and retain moisture.

Easy Tip

Scatter a few seeds between cracks in sidewalks or spaces between flagstones, or in rock walls—sweet alyssum loves warm concrete and stone.

- To help sweet alyssum tolerate drought better, plant in light to medium shade.
- If plants go dormant in the hottest part of summer, shear them back to rejuvenate them.
- This plant reseeds but is not invasive—pull extra seedlings out; they won't resprout.

Pest Control
- Few pests bother sweet alyssum except occasional caterpillars that usually cause little damage.

Complementary Plants
- Plant beneath roses with artemisia for a cottage-garden look.

Recommended Selections
- Deep pink 'Rosie O'Day' is the most fragrant I've grown. A true edger, it grows only 3 inches tall.
- 'Snow Crystals,' which is white and about 6 inches tall, is the most heat-tolerant cultivar I've tried.

Verbena

Verbena species and hybrids

A Sun-Loving Perennial Adored by Butterflies

Plants go in and out of fashion just as clothes do. At the moment, *Verbena canadensis* 'Homestead Purple' is a very popular plant. A vigorous grower covered in purple flower clusters, it's widely used in public gardens. A nice result of the popularity of 'Homestead Purple' is that other rose verbenas—in pink, reddish shades, white, and lavender—are receiving new attention.

Useful Hint

Verbena is an excellent butterfly plant, attracting many species throughout summer.

Top Reasons to Plant

- Tolerates sandy soil
- Drought tolerant
- Long season of bloom
- Reseeds easily
- Few pests or diseases
- Good cut flower
- Attracts butterflies

Bloom Color
Purple, violet, white, or pink

Bloom Period
Spring to fall

Height/Width
6 inches to 3 feet x 3 feet

Planting Location
- Well-drained soil, amended with organic matter to improve drainage if the soil has clay
- Sun

Planting
- Sow seeds or set out plants in spring—both will bloom the first year.
- Space plants 2 feet apart.
- Water well and mulch.

Watering
- Keep soil moist until plants are established.
- Water infrequently but deeply thereafter to encourage drought tolerance.

Fertilizing
- No fertilizer is needed unless plants aren't growing well—too much fertilizer causes excessive, floppy growth.

Suggestions for Vigorous Growth
- Pinch new plants when 6 inches tall and again at 10 inches to encourage branching that increases their airy effect.
- In mass plantings, cut back lightly after each flush of blooms.
- Deadhead flower clusters to promote reblooming.

Easy Tip
Although officially only hardy in warmer states, verbena returned for me in Chattanooga and also seems perennial in the coldest parts of the state. It reseeds prolifically, so plants won't die out.

Pest Control
- Powdery mildew may be a problem in late summer; though it's not attractive, it doesn't seem to harm the plants.

Complementary Plants
- Plant with *Artemisia* 'Powis Castle', coreopsis, Joe-pye weed, and Shasta daisy.

Recommended Selections
- 'Pink Sunrise' has bright-pink flowers on stems rarely taller than 6 inches.
- 'Snowflurry' produces abundant white blooms.
- A popular tall-growing verbena, *Verbena bonariensis* looks so airy it can be used among shorter plants.

Wax Begonia

Begonia Semperflorens-Cultorum hybrids

A Versatile Annual That Grows Almost Anywhere

Is there a more versatile annual than wax begonia? I don't know of any. Wax begonia grows just about anywhere you put it—from full shade beneath a tall oak to blazing sun by the mailbox. The shiny leaves range from bronze to bright-green, providing an accent to red, pink, or white blooms that look at home anywhere in the yard.

Top Reasons to Plant

- Grows well in sun or shade
- Long season of bloom
- Neat edging plant
- Looks good in many settings
- Few serious insect or disease problems

Useful Hint

The Cocktail series—'Gin', 'Whiskey', and 'Vodka'—stands up well to full sun.

Bloom Color
White, pink, or red

Bloom Period
Spring until fall

Height/Width
6 to 14 inches x 6 to 18 inches

Planting Location
- Soil that's rich in organic matter and stays consistently moist
- Partial or full shade preferred, but will grow in full sun with adequate water.

Planting
- Set plants out after threat of frost has passed.
- Add pelleted, slow-release fertilizer to soil at planting.
- Space plants 6 to 12 inches apart depending on mature size.
- Water well and mulch abundantly.

Watering
- Keep well watered throughout the season.

Fertilizing
- Twice monthly, apply a water-soluble fertilizer made for flowering plants.

Suggestions for Vigorous Growth
- Pinch tips back when plants are 4 inches tall to encourage branching and fuller appearance.
- If plants grow leggy, pinch stem tips again.
- Cuttings root easily in water or potting soil.

Easy Tip

Edge evergreen foundation shrubs with a ribbon of red wax begonias.

Pest Control
- Few serious insect or disease problems bother wax begonia.
- Slugs may attack seedlings.
- Overwatering promotes root rot.
- In very dry conditions, whiteflies and spider mites may occur.
- Cut back plants, mulch, and water more often to prevent these insect pests.

Complementary Plants
- Mix plants among perennials in a shady bed to provide color in mid- to late summer, when perennials may have stopped blooming.

Recommended Selections
- The Pizzazz series grows 8 to 12 inches tall and is completely covered with bright-rose, light-pink, red, or white blossoms all summer.
- The Lotto series has the largest flowers.

Yarrow

Achillea species and hybrids

A Perennial with Bright Blooms That Loves Dry, Sunny Spots

Gardeners in our state face two difficult situations. One is spots in the yard that stay constantly wet. The other is dry spots—maybe on a hill, possibly too far from the faucet—in full sun. We wonder what in the world will grow in those places and look good there without any attention. The answer for poor, sunny soils is yarrow, which blooms for a long time, is an excellent cut flower, and dries easily.

Top Reasons to Plant

- Thrives in dry, sunny conditions
- Has unusual flat flower heads
- Attracts butterflies
- Excellent cut flower
- Easy dried flower
- Drought tolerant
- Few insects and diseases
- Good in naturalized settings

Useful Hint

Shade, too much moisture, and too much fertilizer cause stems to fall over instead of growing sturdy and tall.

Bloom Color
Yellow, white, pink, terracotta, orange-red, or gold

Bloom Period
Summer to fall

Height/Width
6 inches to 4 feet x 1 to 4 feet

Planting Location
- Well-drained soil—amend clay with organic matter to improve drainage, but don't add so much the soil becomes too rich
- Sun or a little light shade

Planting
- Set plants out in spring.
- Space plants 2 feet apart.
- Do not mulch.

Watering
- Water sparingly until plants are established.
- In prolonged drought, water only when plants appear to be suffering.

Fertilizing
- No fertilizer is needed unless plants aren't growing well.

Suggestions for Vigorous Growth
- Keep faded flowers picked off.
- Dig up small plants around established clumps in spring and summer and replant right away, watering with a transplant solution.
- If clumps die out in the center, divide them in spring or early fall.

Easy Tip
Cut fully open flowers and hang them upside down indoors in a warm, dry place for easy dried flowers for use in arrangements.

Pest Control
- Fungus diseases—mildew, rust, rot—are occasional problems, especially if plants aren't in full sun and dry soil.
- Mildew and rust are cosmetic problems—cut back the plant if they bother you.

Complementary Plants
- Mix with blue or purple annuals or perennials that don't mind dry soil.
- Grow with purple coneflower, black-eyed Susan, and boltonia.

Recommended Selections
- 'Coronation Gold' never, ever flops over or needs staking—it's completely carefree.

Zinnia

Zinnia species and hybrids

A Wonderful Annual with Lots of Colors, Forms, and Uses

We've come to expect a great deal from annuals. We want them to provide nonstop color from spring until Jack Frost visits in fall. We'd also like them to be available in a host of colors to go with the other flowers in the yard, as well as our indoor decor. Zinnias do all that—and more. Some are great cut flowers, others excel as bedding plants, and others creep along the ground.

Top Reasons to Plant

- Wide range of colors
- Blooms nonstop
- Excellent cut flower
- Good in containers
- Attracts butterflies and hummingbirds
- Easy to grow from seed
- Drought resistant when established

Useful Hint

Both common zinnias and narrowleaf zinnias are staples of the cottage garden, bringing hot colors to tropical plantings.

Bloom Color
Solids and bicolors of white, red, pink, orange, purple, yellow, or green

Bloom Period
Summer until fall

Height/Width
6 inches to 3 feet x 12 inches to 3½ feet

Planting Location
- Average garden soil with only a light addition of compost
- Sun

Planting
- Sow directly in the garden after the soil is warm (May or later)—common zinnia (*Zinnia elegans*) starts easily from seeds.
- Or buy zinnias at garden centers.
- Thin or space the plants so they are 6 to 18 inches apart, depending on mature size.
- Place narrowleaf zinnia (*Zinnia angustifolia*) 8 to 10 inches apart or in containers.
- Water well.
- Mulch lightly, if at all, after the plants are 4 inches tall.

Watering
- Once plants are established, water enough to prevent wilting, but no more.

Fertilizing
- Use a water-soluble fertilizer made for flowering plants—but not more often than every two weeks.

Easy Tip
Choose disease-resistant varieties to avoid leaf fungus, which can only be prevented, not controlled, by chemical fungicides.

Suggestions for Vigorous Growth
- Remove faded flowers from common zinnia regularly.
- Narrowleaf zinnia needs no deadheading.
- To promote more blooms, cut flowers for arrangements often.

Pest Control
- Overwatering, overcrowding, and overcast weather can promote leaf diseases.
- Choose resistant varieties or ask the Extension Service about controls.
- Hot, dry conditions can promote spider mites.
- If spider mites strike, cut flowers from affected stems, remove the plants, and spray the remainder with insecticidal soap.

Complementary Plants
- Make a sunny bed of *Zinnia elegans* with melampodium, marigolds, and gomphrena.

Recommended Selections
- 'Cut and Come Again' remains my favorite for cutting.
- 'Crystal White' and 'Star Gold' are popular narrowleaf zinnias.

Gardening Basics

Gardening isn't difficult; even small children are successful gardeners. But, as with other hobbies, gardening requires paying attention to the basics—soil, water, fertilizer, mulch, and weather. Pay attention to those, and you'll have a landscape to be proud of. Here's what you need to know.

Soil

Soil Is the Foundation

It's hard to get excited about dirt. It's not as interesting as plants. It doesn't bloom; it just sits there, underfoot. But the soil is the foundation for all your gardening. If the soil is good (either naturally or you've improved it), then plants are going to be happy. If the soil is poor, plants won't grow well and will develop problems.

So the first step is to learn what your soil is like. Your nearby neighbors can probably tell you; so can the Soil Conservation Service office in your county. A simple home test is to pick up a golf-ball-sized piece of moist but not wet soil. Squeeze and then release it. If the ball of soil crumbles, it has a balanced texture. If it holds its shape, it's clay.

The Importance of the Right Conditions

If you've read about gardening at all, you've heard the advice about having your soil tested. That's wise counsel. All it involves is digging up small samples of soil from various parts of your yard, mixing them together well, and turning them in to your County Extension Service to be sent off for testing. The best time to do this is fall, when the labs aren't so busy and when—if your soil needs lime—there's plenty of time to apply it and for it to begin to take effect.

When your soil test results come back, you'll learn if your soil is deficient in any nutrients (and consequently what kind and how much fertilizer to use) and also the pH of your soil. What's pH? It's the measure of acidity or alkalinity of your soil. A pH of 7 is neutral—below that is acidic, above that is alkaline. In Tennessee, most of our soils are acidic, but some of us do live on properties with alkaline soil. Because plants have definite preferences for one type or the other, it's important to know your soil's pH level.

Because the ideal soil for most plants is moist and well drained, it's good to know whether your soil tends to stay wet or dry and whether it drains well. Clay soils stay wet longer than loam; sandy or rocky soils drain much faster than other types of soil—which is often good—but they need watering more frequently. Plants that are able to live in especially wet or dry conditions are noted in the descriptions throughout this book.

If you suspect that drainage is poor at a site in your yard, test to be sure. Dig a hole 6 to 12 inches deep and as wide. Fill the hole with water and time how long it takes for the water to drain completely. If it takes

15 minutes to half an hour, drainage is good. Faster means the soil doesn't hold moisture well, and slower means clay.

Improving Your Soil

Just because your yard has a particular type of soil doesn't mean you have to live with it. Instead, improve it with soil amendments. Organic matter, such as compost, not only lightens heavy clay soil and improves its drainage, but it also boosts the water-holding capability of lighter soil.

Other good soil amendments include rotted leaves, rotted sawdust, composted manure, fine bark, old mushroom compost, and peat moss.

If you're digging a new bed, spread 3 or more inches of compost or other soil amendment on top of the soil and till it into the top 8 inches of soil. Otherwise, improve the soil as you plant.

Water

How Much Is Enough?

The rule of thumb says most popular garden plants need 1 inch of water per week in the growing season, and many need its equivalent all year long. Unfortunately, the amount of rain that fell at your city's airport, or other official weather station, may not be the amount that fell on your plants. The only way to know for sure is to put up a rain gauge to assist in obtaining a specific measurement. In summer, when "scattered showers" are always in the forecast, I find that the "official" rainfall and what fell on my yard are rarely the same. If I had watered—or not watered—on the basis of the totals given by the National Weather Service, I would almost always either overwater or under-water my plants. Instead, I save time and money—as well as protect my plants—by knowing exactly how much rainfall they receive.

When and How to Water

In general, plants respond best to thorough but occasional soakings rather than daily spurts of smaller amounts of water. Regulate water pressure to reduce runoff so more water gets into the soil. Such good garden practices as these encourage plants to develop deeper roots, which provide greater stability; that's especially important for shrubs and trees. Deep roots also make plants more drought-tolerant.

The worst thing you can do for your plants in a drought is to stand over them with a hose for a few minutes each evening. Most of the water runs off instead of soaking in, and what does penetrate the soil doesn't usually go deeply enough. The soil should be wet to at least 8 to 10 inches deep for perennials and other flowers; 12 to 24 inches deep for trees and shrubs. Insert a dry stick into the soil to be sure how far the water has penetrated. It's impossible to say how long watering will take, because water absorption rates vary by soil type. An inch of water will penetrate fastest into sandy soil and slowest into clay. Time your watering the first few times and then you'll have a guide for future watering.

If you use sprinklers or an irrigation system, set out coffee cans at intervals to measure the amount of water delivered in 30 minutes. That will show you how long it will take the system to deliver an inch of water to your plants.

Too little water causes plants to perform poorly. Small leaves, pale or no flowers, stunted size, wilting, little or no fruit formation, and premature leaf drop can all be signs of water stress. Soil surfaces may dry out and even crack, destroying feeder roots near the surface; their loss can be fatal to annual flowers and vegetables. If watering seems adequate and plants still wilt daily, they may be located in too much sun. If such beds are deeply mulched, check to be certain that the water is getting down into the soil.

The best time of day to water is early morning; late afternoon is second best. No one wants to get up at 4 a.m. to turn on a lawn sprinkler. But there's an easy way out. Water timers can be attached to any hose and faucet to regulate sprinklers and soaker hoses; their effective use is the hallmark of in-ground irrigation systems. Soaker hoses—which don't wet foliage—may be used any time day or night.

The Right Tools

As with all gardening activities, watering is more efficient with the right equipment. Small gardens and containers of plants can be watered efficiently with only a garden hose and watering can—use a water-breaking nozzle to convert the solid stream of water into smaller droplets that will not damage plants. When watering container plants, irrigate until water flows out the drain hole in the bottom of the pot, and then cover the soil with water once again. This practice keeps the root zone healthy by exchanging gases in the soil.

Larger garden beds require sprinklers, either portable or in-ground systems. Sprinklers spread plenty of water around and most of it gets to soil level; the rest is lost to evaporation but does provide a playground and essential moisture for birds. Adjustable sprinkler heads are a good investment; the ability to set the pattern specifically to increase the size of the water droplets gives the gardener more control over irrigation.

Where water is precious or pricey, drip watering systems and soaker hoses offer very efficient irrigation. They're especially useful around plants, such as roses and zinnias, that develop mildew or other fungus diseases easily. These hoses apply much smaller amounts of water at one time than you may be used to. To measure output, let the water run for an hour, then turn the soaker hose off. Dig down into the soil to see how deeply it is wet. That will help you gauge how long to keep soaker hoses or drip systems on. For the health of your plants, when watering this way, occasionally supplement with overhead watering (either sprinklers or hand-held hoses) to clean the leaves and deter insects.

Watering Plants in Containers

Because hanging baskets and annuals in small pots often become rootbound by midsummer—when temperature and humidity levels are high—they may need watering once or even twice daily. You can lessen this chore slightly by mixing a super-absorbent polymer into the soil at planting time. When mixed, these look like Jell-O®. They absorb moisture, and then release it as the plants need it. Although they're pricey, only a tiny amount is needed (never use more than what is recommended, or you'll have a mess on your hands), and they last in the soil for up to five years. My experience is that they just about double the length of time between waterings. That is, if I would water a container plant without the polymer once a day, then with the polymer, I can usually water every other day. That may not sound like a big deal, but in the dog days of August it's a blessing! These super-absorbent polymers are sold under a number of trade names; ask for them at garden centers and nurseries.

Why Is Watering Important?

Water is vital because it makes up at least 95 percent of a plant's mass, and its timely supply is crucial to healthy growth. It is literally the elixir of life, moving from the root zone and leaf surfaces into the plant's systems, carrying nutrients and filling cells to create stems, leaves, flowers, and fruit. Without ample water for roots to work efficiently, nutrients go unabsorbed, growth is stunted, and plant tissues eventually collapse, wilt, and die. Ironically, too much water creates equally disastrous conditions. When soils are flooded, the roots suffocate, stop pumping water and nutrients, and the plant eventually dies.

Watering Tips

- Shrubs and other plants growing under the overhang of the roof may need more frequent watering than those planted out in the yard. Foundation shrubs often don't get much water from precipitation, and they also have to contend with the reflected heat from the house.
- Raised beds, berms, and mounds also need watering more often.
- Watch out for excessive runoff when watering. If the soil isn't absorbing the moisture, slow down the rate of water application.
- Never fertilize without watering thoroughly afterward. Fertilizer salts can damage the roots if moisture is lacking.

Fertilizer

Nutrition in appropriate amounts is as important as sunlight and water to plant growth. Three elements—nitrogen, phosphorus, and potassium—

are essential to plants and are called macronutrients. Some of these nutrients are obtained from the soil, but if they're not available in the amounts needed, the gardener must provide them through fertilizer.

The Role of Nutrition

Each nutrient plays a major role in plant development. Nitrogen produces healthy, green leaves, while phosphorus and potassium are responsible for strong stems, flowers, and fruit. Without enough of any one of the macronutrients, plants falter and often die. Other elements, needed in much smaller amounts, are known as *trace elements, minor elements,* or *micronutrients.* Included in most complete fertilizers, the minor elements are boron, iron, manganese, zinc, copper, and molybdenum.

Fertilizers come from two basic sources: organic materials and manufactured ones. Organic sources include rocks, plants, and animals; fertilizers are extracted or composted from them. The advantages of organics affect both plants and people: centuries of history to explain their uses, slow and steady action on plants and especially soils, and the opportunity to put local and recycled materials to good use. Manufactured sources are the products of laboratories. Nutrients are formulated by scientists and produced in factories. The advantages of commercially prepared inorganic fertilizers are consistency of product, formula diversity, definitive analysis of contents, and ready availability. Most gardeners use a combination of the two, but purely organic enthusiasts use natural products exclusively.

Speaking the Language

Every fertilizer sold must have a label detailing its contents. Understanding the composition and numbers improves the gardener's ability to provide nutrition. The three numbers on a fertilizer label relate to its contents; the first number indicates the amount of nitrogen, the second number the amount of phosphorus, and the third the amount of potassium. For example, if the numbers are 20-15-10, it means the product has 20 percent nitrogen, 15 percent phosphorus, and 10 percent potassium. Their relative numbers reveal their impact on plants—a formula high in nitrogen greens-up the plant and grows leaves, ones with lower first and higher second and third numbers encourage flowers and fruits.

A good rule of thumb is to use a balanced fertilizer (one where all the numbers are equal, as in 10-10-10) to prepare new soil. Then fertilize the plants with a formula higher in nitrogen at the beginning of the growing season to get plants up and growing; switch to special formulas (that is, those formulated specifically for flowers and fruiting) later in the season.

Fertilizers can be water-soluble or granular; both types have advantages and appropriate uses. Soluble formulas are mixed in water. They are available in very specific formulas, compact to store, fast acting, and can be used either as a soil drench or to spray the leaves (plants will absorb them through foliage or soil). Solubles work quickly (leaves will often green up overnight—great if you want the yard to look good for a cookout), but their effects do not last long and they must be reapplied frequently. They are especially useful in growing container plants, which need more frequent watering as well as fertilizing.

Granular fertilizers can be worked into the soil when tilling or used as a top dressing around established plants. They incorporate easily into soils, and their effects may last for several weeks. Slow-release fertilizers, which are usually pelleted, keep working for three to nine months depending on the formula. The coated pellets of these popular fertilizers (with names like Osmocote, Polyon, and Once) decompose slowly with water or temperature changes over time. They cost more than granular fertilizers but save much time for the gardener because they're usually applied just once a season. Their other big advantage over granular fertilizers is that it's almost impossible for gardeners to "burn" plant foliage when using them; whereas, great care must be taken to keep granular fertilizers off plant parts.

Organic fertilizers also work very slowly, over a long period of time. They usually have lower ratios of active ingredients (nitrogen, phosphorus, and potassium) and so provide steady nutrition, rather than a quick green-up. Organic fertilizers that provide nitrogen are bloodmeal, fishmeal, soybean meal, and cottonseed meal. Organic phosphorous fertilizers include bonemeal and rock phosphate. To provide potassium, use greensand or sulfate of potash-magnesia.

Although soil may contain many nutrients, most gardeners find applying fertilizer makes growing plants more satisfactory. However, many tend to overdo it. Too much fertilizer can harm plants, just as too little does. Excessive nitrogen often leads to attacks of aphids, which appreciate the tender young growth that's being produced, and to floppy stems in perennial plants.

Rules to Remember

- Never fertilize a dry plant. Water the day before you fertilize at least, or several hours before.
- Always use products at the recommended rate or a bit lower. Never use more than what is recommended.
- Rinse stray granules off plant leaves to prevent burning.

Mulch

One important thing you can provide your plants—which may mean the difference between success and failure—is mulch.

Mulch Matters

Mulch is the most useful material in your garden. A blanket of mulch keeps soil warmer in winter and cooler in summer, prevents erosion, and doesn't allow the soil surface to develop a hard crust. When heavy rain or drought causes water stress, mulch ameliorates both situations, acting as a barrier to flooding and conserving water in dry soil. Mulch suppresses weed growth and prevents soil from splashing onto leaves (and thus reduces the spread of soilborne diseases). A neat circle of mulch around newly planted trees offers a physical barrier to keep lawnmowers and string trimmers away from tender trunks. (Such trunk damage is one of the leading causes of death for young trees.) Mulch also makes a garden look neater than it does with just bare soil.

What Mulch Is

Mulch can be any material, organic or inorganic, that covers the soil's surface. Popular organic mulches include hardwood barks (ground, shredded, or nuggets), pine and wheat straws, shredded leaves and leaf mold, and shredded newsprint and other papers. Your excess grass clippings also make a great mulch, provided you let them age a week or so (until they're no longer hot) before using, so they don't burn plants. Organic mulches gradually break down and enrich the soil.

If you can find a source of free organic material in your area—peanut hulls, ground-up corncobs, waste from an old cotton gin, or similar materials—so much the better. I have a friend who's a high school industrial arts teacher, and several times a year he brings me enormous bags of sawdust, left over from his students' projects. Some of it I let rot and use as a soil amendment, but I also spread quite a bit of the fresh sawdust around all sorts of plants as mulch.

And, of course, don't overlook rotted leaves as an excellent no-cost mulch. I've often wondered why some homeowners lug bags of leaves to the curb in fall, then, in spring, turn around and spend money to buy bags and bales of mulch material from a nursery.

Inorganic mulches can be made from pea gravel, crushed lava rock, marble chips, crushed pottery chards, and clear or black plastic. Also available in garden centers to be used as mulch are rolls of landscape fabric, which look like a thick cloth. Both plastic and landscape fabric need to be covered with a layer of an organic mulch for appearance's sake, unless used in the vegetable garden.

In general, organic mulches are best around your yard's ornamental plantings. Black plastic and some landscape fabrics can prevent air, water, and nutrients from readily reaching the roots of your plants. They also cause shallow root growth, which makes the plants more susceptible to drought.

Because pea gravel and other stone mulches are difficult to move if you decide you don't like the way they look, you may want to try them in a small spot first. They're ideal, however, for pathways and other permanent areas, because they don't rot or float away.

What Can Mulch Do?

Beyond practical considerations, you may want to think about what different mulch materials offer the landscape aesthetically. The color and texture of many mulches can be attractive and offer contrast to green plants and lawns. Used on walkways and paths, mulch should provide a comfortable walking surface in addition to adding color and weed control to high-traffic areas. Mulch adds definition to planting areas and can be extended to neatly cover thinning lawn areas under trees. Mulch also works as a landscape-unifying element—use the same mulch material throughout the garden to tie diverse plantings together visually and to reduce maintenance at the same time.

Mulch Dos and Don'ts

- Apply mulch 3 inches deep when planting new trees and shrubs.
- Replenish mulch around perennials each year when tending established beds in spring or fall. Apply pine straw to a depth of about 5 inches because it quickly settles.
- Use pine straw to mulch plantings on slopes or hills, where other mulches may be washed away in hard rains.
- Don't pile mulch against a plant's stem or trunk; that can cause damage. Instead, start spreading mulch about 2 inches away from the plant.
- Don't pile mounds of mulch around trees; it's not good for them.
- When setting out small bedding plants, you may find it easier to mulch the entire bed first—then dig individual holes—rather than to try to spread mulch evenly around tiny seedlings.
- Don't spread mulch over weed-infested ground, thinking it will kill the weeds. Generally, they'll pop right through. Instead, weed before mulching.
- Add to the organic mulch around each plant yearly—9 to 12 months after you originally mulched. Think of this mulch renewal not as a chore, but as a garden job that pays rich dividends.
- In fall always add more mulch around plants that may be damaged by an extra-cold winter.
- Wait until the soil has reliably warmed up (usually in May sometime) before mulching heat-loving plants, such as perennial hibiscus, caladium, and Madagascar periwinkle. If they're mulched too early, the soil will remain cool and they'll get off to a very slow start.
- Don't mulch ground that stays wet all the time.
- Don't over-do the mulch. More than 4 or 5 inches of mulch may prevent water from penetrating to the soil below.

Glossary

Alkaline soil: soil with a pH greater than 7.0. It lacks acidity, often because it has limestone in it.

All-purpose fertilizer: powdered, liquid, or granular fertilizer with a balanced proportion of the three key nutrients—nitrogen (N), phosphorus (P), and potassium (K). It is suitable for maintenance nutrition for most plants.

Annual: a plant that lives its entire life in one season. It is genetically determined to germinate, grow, flower, set seed, and die the same year.

Balled and burlapped: describes a tree or shrub grown in the field whose soilball was wrapped with protective burlap and twine when the plant was dug up to be sold or transplanted.

Bare root: describes plants that have been packaged without any soil around their roots. (Often young shrubs and trees purchased through the mail arrive with their exposed roots covered with moist peat or sphagnum moss, sawdust, or similar material, and wrapped in plastic.)

Barrier plant: a plant that has intimidating thorns or spines and is sited purposely to block foot traffic or other access to the home or yard.

Beneficial insects: insects or their larvae that prey on pest organisms and their eggs. They may be flying insects, such as ladybugs, parasitic wasps, praying mantids, and soldier bugs, or soil dwellers such as predatory nematodes, spiders, and ants.

Berm: a narrow, raised ring of soil around a tree, used to hold water so it will be directed to the root zone.

Bract: a modified leaf structure on a plant stem near its flower, resembling a petal. Often it is more colorful and visible than the actual flower, as in dogwood.

Bud union: the place where the top of a plant was grafted to the rootstock; usually refers to roses.

Canopy: the overhead branching area of a tree, usually referring to its extent including foliage.

Cold hardiness: the ability of a perennial plant to survive the winter cold in a particular area.

Composite: a flower that is actually composed of many tiny flowers. Typically, they are flat clusters of tiny, tight florets, sometimes surrounded by wider-petaled florets. Composite flowers are highly attractive to bees and beneficial insects.

Compost: organic matter that has undergone progressive decomposition by microbial and macrobial activity until it is reduced to a spongy, fluffy texture. Added to soil of any type, it improves the soil's ability to hold air and water and to drain well.

Corm: the swollen energy-storing structure, analogous to a bulb, under the soil at the base of the stem of plants such as crocus and gladiolus.

Crown: the base of a plant at, or just beneath, the surface of the soil where the roots meet the stems.

Cultivar: a CULTIvated VARiety. It is a naturally occurring form of a plant that has been identified as special or superior and is purposely selected for propagation and production.

Deadhead: a pruning technique that removes faded flower heads from plants to improve their appearances, abort seed production, and stimulate further flowering.

Deciduous plants: unlike evergreens, these trees and shrubs lose their leaves in the fall.

Desiccation: drying out of foliage tissues, usually due to drought or wind.

Division: the practice of splitting apart perennial plants to create several smaller-rooted segments. The practice is useful for controlling the plant's size and for acquiring more plants; it is also essential to the health and continued flowering of certain ones.

Dormancy: the period, usually the winter, when perennial plants temporarily cease active growth and rest. Dormant is the verb form, as used in this sentence: *Some plants, like spring-blooming bulbs, go dormant in the summer.*

Established: the point at which a newly planted tree, shrub, or flower begins to produce new growth, either foliage or stems. This is an indication that the roots have recovered from transplant shock and have begun to grow and spread.

Evergreen: perennial plants that do not lose their foliage annually with the onset of winter. Needled or broadleaf foliage will persist and continues to function on a plant through one or more winters, aging and dropping unobtrusively in cycles of three or four years or more.

Floret: a tiny flower, usually one of many forming a cluster, that comprises a single blossom.

Foliar: of or about foliage—usually refers to the practice of spraying foliage, as in fertilizing or treating with insecticide; leaf tissues absorb liquid directly for fast results, and the soil is not affected.

Germinate: to sprout. Germination is a fertile seed's first stage of development.

Graft (union): the point on the stem of a woody plant with sturdier roots where a stem from a highly ornamental plant is inserted so that it will join with it. Roses are commonly grafted.

Hands: the female flowers on a banana tree; they turn into bananas.

Hardscape: the permanent, structural, nonplant part of a landscape, such as walls, sheds, pools, patios, arbors, and walkways.

Herbaceous: plants having fleshy or soft stems that die back with frost; the opposite of woody.

Hybrid: a plant that is the result of intentional or natural cross-pollination between two or more plants of the same species or genus.

Low water demand: describes plants that tolerate dry soil for varying periods of time. Typically, they have succulent, hairy, or silvery-gray foliage and tuberous roots or taproots.

Mulch: a layer of material over bare soil to protect it from erosion and compaction by rain, and to discourage weeds. It may be inorganic (gravel, fabric) or organic (wood chips, bark, pine needles, chopped leaves).

Naturalize: (*a*) to plant seeds, bulbs, or plants in a random, informal pattern as they would appear in their natural habitats; (*b*) to adapt to and spread throughout adopted habitats (a tendency of some nonnative plants).

Nectar: the sweet fluid produced by glands on flowers that attract pollinators such as hummingbirds and honeybees, for whom it is a source of energy.

Organic material, organic matter: any material or debris that is derived from plants. It is carbon-based material capable of undergoing decomposition and decay.

Peat moss: organic matter from peat sedges (United States) or sphagnum mosses (Canada), often used to improve soil texture. The acidity of sphagnum peat moss makes it ideal for boosting or maintaining soil acidity while also improving its drainage.

Perennial: a flowering plant that lives over two or more seasons. Many die back with frost, but their roots survive the winter and generate new shoots in the spring.

pH: a measurement of the relative acidity (low pH) or alkalinity (high pH) of soil or water based on a scale of 1 to 14, 7 being neutral. Individual plants require soil to be within a certain range so that nutrients can dissolve in moisture and be available to them.

Pinch: to remove tender stems and/or leaves by pressing them between thumb and forefinger. This pruning technique encourages branching, compactness, and flowering in plants, or it removes aphids clustered at growing tips.

Pollen: the yellow, powdery grains in the center of a flower. A plant's male sex cells, they are transferred to the female plant parts by means of wind or animal pollinators to fertilize them and create seeds.

Raceme: an arrangement of single-stalked flowers along an elongated, unbranched axis.

Rhizome: a swollen energy-storing stem structure, similar to a bulb, that lies horizontally in the soil, with roots emerging from its lower surface and growth shoots from a growing point at or near its tip, as in bearded iris.

Rootbound (or potbound): the condition of a plant that has been confined in a container too long, its roots having been forced to wrap around themselves and even swell out of the container. Successful transplanting or repotting requires untangling and trimming away of some of the matted roots.

Root flare: the transition at the base of a tree trunk where the bark tissue begins to differentiate and roots begin to form just before entering the soil. This area should not be covered with soil when planting a tree.

Self-seeding: the tendency of some plants to sow their seeds freely around the yard. It creates many seedlings the following season that may or may not be welcome.

Semievergreen: tending to be evergreen in a mild climate but deciduous in a rigorous one.

Shearing: the pruning technique whereby plant stems and branches are cut uniformly with long-bladed pruning shears (hedge shears) or powered hedge trimmers. It is used when creating and maintaining hedges and topiary.

Slow-acting fertilizer: fertilizer that is water insoluble and therefore releases its nutrients gradually as a function of soil temperature, moisture, and related microbial activity. Typically granular, it may be organic or synthetic.

Succulent growth: the sometimes undesirable production of fleshy, water-storing leaves or stems that results from overfertilization.

Sucker: a new-growing shoot. Underground plant roots produce suckers to form new stems and spread by means of these suckering roots to form large plantings, or colonies. Some plants produce root suckers or branch suckers as a result of pruning or wounding.

Tuber: a type of underground storage structure in a plant stem, analogous to a bulb. It generates roots below and stems above ground (example: dahlia).

Variegated: having various colors or color patterns. The term usually refers to plant foliage that is streaked, edged, blotched, or mottled with a contrasting color—often green with yellow, cream, or white.

White grubs: fat, off-white, wormlike larvae of Japanese beetles. They reside in the soil and feed on plant (especially grass) roots until summer when they emerge as beetles to feed on plant foliage.

Wings: (*a*) the corky tissue that forms edges along the twigs of some woody plants such as winged euonymus; (*b*) the flat, dried extension of tissue on some seeds, such as maple, that catch the wind and help them disseminate.

Bibliography

Reference Books

Armitage, Allan M. *Herbaceous Perennial Plants.* Champaign, Illinois: Stipes Publishing, 1997.

Bender, Steve, editor. *The Southern Living Garden Problem Solver.* Birmingham, Alabama: Oxmoor House, 1999.

Darke, Rick. *Color Encyclopedia of Ornamental Grasses.* Portland, Oregon: Timber Press, 1999.

Dirr, Michael A. *Manual of Woody Landscape Plants.* Champaign, Illinois: Stipes Publishing, 1998.

DiSabito-Aust, Tracy. *The Well-Tended Perennial Garden.* Portland, Oregon: Timber Press, 1998.

Heriteau, Jacqueline and Marc Cathey, editors. *The National Arboretum Book of Outstanding Garden Plants.* New York, New York: Simon & Schuster, 1990.

Hoshizaki, Barbara Joe and Robbin C. Moran. *Fern Grower's Manual.* Portland, Oregon: Timber Press, 2001.

General Reading

Bender, Steve and Felder Rushing. *Passalong Plants.* Chapel Hill, North Carolina: The University of North Carolina Press, 1993.

Hodgson, Larry. *Perennials for Every Purpose.* Emmaus, Pennsylvania: Rodale Press, 2000.

Holmes, Roger, editor. *Taylor's Guide to Ornamental Grasses.* Boston, Massachusetts: Houghton Mifflin Co., 1997.

Ogden, Scott. *Garden Bulbs for the South.* Dallas, Texas: Taylor Publishing, 1994.

Roth, Susan A. *The Four-Season Landscape.* Emmaus, Pennsylvania: Rodale Press, 1994.

Sedenko, Jerry. *The Butterfly Garden.* New York, New York: Villard Books, 1991.

Xerces Society, The, and The Smithsonian Institution. *Butterfly Gardening.* San Francisco, California: Sierra Club Books, 1998.

Photography Credits

Thomas Eltzroth: pages 9, 10, 14, 18, 22, 24, 38, 40, 42, 46, 48, 52, 54, 56, 58, 60, 64, 66, 70, 72, 78, 82, 84, 92, 94, 96, 98, 102, 106

Jerry Pavia: pages 20, 30, 36, 50, 62, 74, 76, 86, 88, 104, 108, 110

Liz Ball and Rick Ray: pages 11, 12, 26, 28, 32, 44, 68, 100

Andre Viette: pages 8, 80

Pam Harper: page 90

Felder Rushing: page 34

Dency Kane: page 16

Plant Index

Want to know more about Tennessee gardening?

Interested in terrific trees for Tennessee? Do you want healthful and tasty herbs, fruits, and vegetables from your Tennessee garden? How about stunning Tennessee shrubs?

If you enjoy *50 Great Flowers for Tennessee*, you will appreciate similar books featuring Tennessee trees, vegetables (including fruits and herbs), and shrubs. These valuable books also deserve a place in your gardening library.

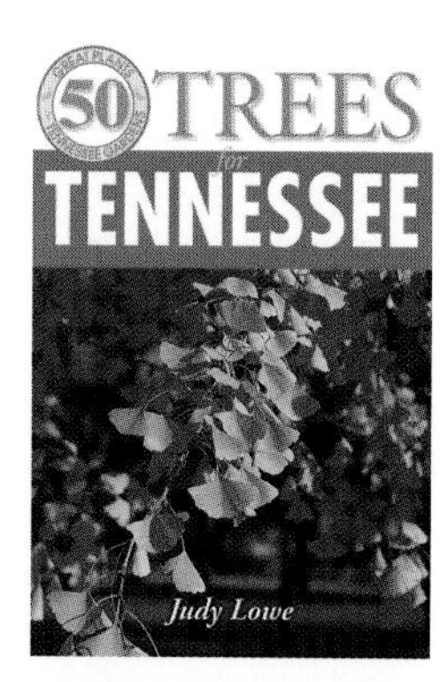

50 Great Trees for Tennessee

Author Judy Lowe recommends fifty great trees for Tennessee. She offers fantastic options on small flowering trees, great evergreens, and trees that delight with multiseason interest.

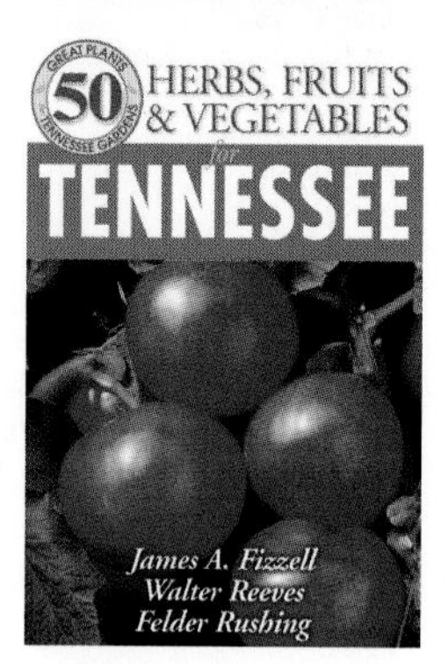

50 Great Herbs, Fruits and Vegetables for Tennessee

If you are inclined to "edibles" in your Tennessee garden, this is the book for you. It provides valuable advice on how to select, plant, and grow tasty herbs, luscious fruits, and flavorful vegetables. Written by James A. Fizzell, Walter Reeves, and Felder Rushing, this book offers more than seventy-five years of gardening wisdom all in an easy-to-use format.

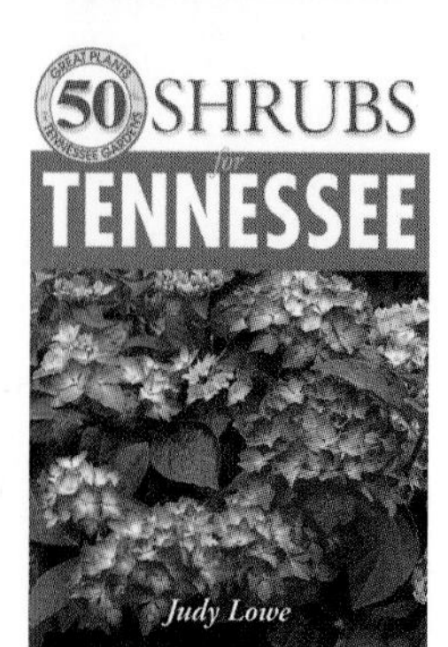

50 Great Shrubs for Tennessee

If you want guidance on great shrubs for Tennessee, this is the book for you. From the boxwood to the flowering azalea, Judy Lowe shares her gardening wit and wisdom on fifty wonderful shrubs for Tennessee.

Look for each of these books today.